Decorative Needlecraft

Decorative Needlecraft

Edited by Allen D. Bragdon

Watson-Guptill Publications
New York

Editor: Allen D. Bragdon
Editorial Production: Carolyn Walsh Zellers
Cover Design: John B. Miller, For Art Sake, Inc.

First published in 1994 by Watson-Guptill Publications,
a division of BPI Communications, Inc.,
1515 Broadway, New York, NY 10036

Library of Congress Cataloging-in Publication Data

Decorative Needlecraft / edited by Allen D. Bragdon.
        p.   cm.
    ISBN 0-8230-1264-6
    1. Needlework—Patterns. I. Bragdon, Allen D.
    TT753.D43   1994
    746.4—dc20   94-14203
                                      CIP

Distributed in the United Kingdom by
Phaidon Press, Ltd., 140 Kensington Church Street,
London W8 4BN, England.

Distributed in Europe (except the United Kingdom),
South and Central America, the Caribbean, the Far
East, the Southeast, and Central Asia by Rotovision
S.A., Route Suisse 9, CH-1295 Mies, Switzerland.

Printed in South Korea

First printing, 1994.

1 2 3 4 5 6 7 8 9

02 01 00 99 98 97 96 95 94

CREDITS & ACKNOWLEDGMENTS

Page 10: *Decorative Embroidery Stitches* worked
by Carolyn E.R. Reenstra.

Page 33: *Crib Crazy Quilt* from the permanent
collection of the Museum of American Folk Art,
gift of Margaret Cavigga.

Pages 38 & 39: *Dorothy Allen Sampler* courtesy of
Bennington Museum, Bennington, VT.

Pages 40 & 41: *Birth Sampler* designed by
Carolyn E.R. Reenstra.

Page 43: *Sampler Sayings,* from the collection of
M. Finkel & Daughter, 936 Pine St., Philadelphia,
PA 19107.

Page 46: *Picture Framing* written by Lisa Clark.

Pages 52-54, 72-74: *Seascape Bib, Child's Pullover,
Ducklings* and *Piglets* designs from the collection
of Lisbeth Perrone.

Page 56: *Evening Collar and Bag* worked by Diane
Piette.

Pages 58 to 61: *Reticules* courtesy of Centerville
Historical Society, Centerville, MA.

Page 63: *Doorstop Cat* canvas painted by Melinda
McAra; stitched by The Osterville Needlepoint
Shop; finished by The Binding Stitch, Dennis,
MA.

Page 64: *Navajo Needlepoint Pillow* stitched by
Ellen Nadler for Sundance Designs, Tucson AZ.

Pages 66 to 71: Carousel figures from the
Youree, Stevens, Abbott, and Daniel collections,
as reproduced in *Painted Ponies*, Zon
International Publishing Company.

Page 76: *Wampanoag Bracelet* beaded by Alice
Lopez of the Massachusetts Wampanoag tribe.

Page 78: *Dollhouse Rugs*: stenciled floor cloth by
Tillie Sobieski; hooked and braided rugs by
Liddie Radcliffe.

Page 86: *Huck Embroidery* towels stitched by
Diane Piette.

Pages 100-110: *Teddy Bear Boutique* designs created and stitched by Marsha Evans Moore.

The projects in this volume have been selected
from *American Pastimes*, an 18-volume work on
traditional folk handcraft techniques and designs
edited by Allen D. Bragdon.

EDITOR'S PREFACE

This book offers three things to stitchers who use their art for decorative embellishment and who prefer to work with traditional designs and materials.

First, you will find a treasury of old embroidery stitches with diagrams showing how to execute them. If you have never done any embroidery work at all you had best find a friend who can show you the basics. From there our instructions can act as a reminder and will help you expand your repertoire.

You may find that we have named some stitches perhaps differently from the way you know them. Like many folk traditions — the designs for quilting squares, for example — the names hung on stitches change depending on what century and county you come from.

Second, we show how you might apply traditional stitching techniques from commonly known cross-stitch, needlepoint, crochet and knitting, to less known huck, trapunto, and monogramming with openwork hems.

Third, we have provided step-by-step instructions for making over 30 classic projects that use the stitching techniques shown. These include detailed materials lists, charts and full-size patterns as required. Most projects are quite simple, and useful, and make charming gifts.

Please use this book both as a source for traditional designs and techniques that have worked over time and as a source of inspiration for creating your own variations. In that sense it is a source of ideas to adapt to your own taste in color, your preference for size, and the materials that you have available.

Often the most exciting results of creative effort come from some original way of combining elements or a lucky accident—which, not incidentally, accounts for the charming appeal of most folk art. (After all, *someone* had to invent each one of the decorative stitches we now use.) As an old Kentucky quilter once put it: "God gives you the pieces, but it's up to you how you put them together."

Now to some housekeeping details:

About Patterns: We have spared you the tedium of enlarging designs printed small on grids because that method is frustrating, often inaccurate, and now out of date. Instead, we have supplied the patterns full size, usually on fold-out sheets that are perforated along their bound-in edge so you can tear them out neatly without damaging the book.

Iron-on Transfers: On one of the large sheets the patterns are printed with a special heat-transfer ink that melts when the paper is heated by ironing it. These designs are printed in reverse so you can lay them, ink-side down, onto fabric or onto cardboard for templates or paper for patterns. Iron the back of the paper with a dry iron as you would for a delicate fabric (hotter for transferring onto dark-colored material). Although the design will transfer more than once, use it to make one permanent template—of cardboard, for example—for cutting patterns, rather than ironing the pattern onto the fabric each time you use it.

Copying: Photocopy or trace the smaller patterns printed on the book pages so they will be more convenient to work from. Almost all copy shops now can copy directly from your book page, and even enlarge or reduce whatever is printed on it to any size you want.

We herewith give you legal permission to make a photocopy of any of our patterns and designs for your own use (not to sell). If you want to make multiple copies for a school class, please write to the publisher (the address is on the facing page) and they will try to work something out.

Hints: ❈ *Whenever we know of a shortcut, an alternate way to do something, a caution about a tricky part or some other bit of advice, we have printed it in italic type, like this, with that little symbol at the beginning.*

Designs and Materials: We selected designs that have been used traditionally and have proven their appeal over the years. Many of these designs have appeared in museum collections, or in old records and other books. We have reproduced them here, along with the instructions and stitches used to recreate them, because they represent traditions worth preserving. We listed the materials and tools needed for each project in the order you will use them when you assemble it.

We placed a color photo or drawing of each finished project next to the instructions, which usually face it and sometimes continue on the next page. The title of each project appears next to the page number on the right-hand page. The name of the chapter is printed in capital letters next to the page number on the left-hand page.

Most of the designs and all the techniques in this book have been passed down through someone's family. As a child we remember our mother occasionally pointing out a piece of needlework to us, naming the relation or friend who had worked it, and telling us something about them. Some pieces were her work as a child. Most had been passed down through two or more generations. Our children will have them someday too. It helps the past seem real — and more precious somehow.

— Allen D. Bragdon, Editor

CONTENTS

STITCHES & SAMPLERS

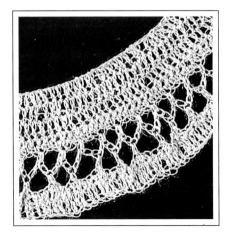

CLOTHING, ACCESSORIES & HOME DECOR

"Hannah Reed is my name New England is my Nation BOSTON is my dwelling place and Christ is my salvation. . . ."

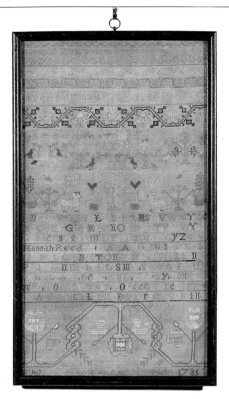

Left: *The work of Hannah Reed, dated 1735, is a classic example of why samplers were initially called "examplers." They served as important references for showing how various embroidery stitches were worked. After finishing her exampler, a young woman would roll it up to store in a drawer—like a reference book in a bookcase—until she needed to know how a particular stitch looked. Often, Englishmen would be called upon to teach the young women, and in doing so, defined sampler-making as a very prim, precise skill with no room for self-expression. Because the counting of stitches for each line was required, it was also a rigorous mathematical exercise. Hannah Reed's contains bands of two uppercase alphabets and one lowercase, along with birds, hearts, crowns and sheep. Measuring 10½ inches wide by 18½ inches high, her sampler illustrates a superb command of each stitch.*

Below: *When Elizabeth Crosthwaite was 12 years old, just before the Civil War, a sampler was used as a teaching tool to instruct little girls in their letters and numbers. After they had learned to stitch the alphabet and the border, they could try their own designs. In the early days, when pattern books did not exist, traditional themes were handed down from mother to daughter. Houses, flowers, birds and pets were popular. Her superbly executed sampler contains many of these traditional elements and motifs.*

"Go on I pray and Let Me Still Pursue Those Golden Arts The Vulgar Never Knew"

Above: *After 1750, as the printing press became increasingly accessible and books affordable, it became more common for young women to learn how to read. Therefore, the exampler evolved into the more pictorial sampler. Isabella Hempstock's shows needlework that is remarkable not only in its quality but in the quantity and variety of stitches executed. Measuring 12 inches wide by 15½ inches high, it is dated 1776 and is probably of English origin.*

Stitches & Samplers

As you explore this treasury of decorative stitches we expect you will find among them both variations on old friends and opportunities to make new ones. This chapter provides stitchers with resources they can turn to again and again.

Among these references are:

- Full-color, life-sized photos and diagrams for 34 different embroidery stitches.

- Four charted alphabets to stitch monograms or some of the 30 motifs from antique samplers.

- Three complete samplers to copy from charts with exact color matches to the antique originals (Dorothy Allen's sampler is 260 years old).

- Easy-to-follow diagrams for crochet and knitting stitches, casting, etc.

- Detailed instructions for blocking, matting and framing your finished work.

Decorative Embroidery Stitches

In the old days, invention was the necessity of mothers when printed fabrics cost a lot and the days were drab with repetitious labors. Decorative embroidery filled a need all people feel for pattern and bright color. In the parlors of Victorian ladies, young women practiced the stitches they learned at finishing schools. A Victorian crazy quilt, like the one pictured on page 30, was often a sample of an embroiderer's versatility and inventiveness. The stitches on the pages that follow are some old favorites and a few new twists of the needle stitched for us by a master embroiderer who shares the following hints: Make sure you don't pull stitches too tight or leave them too loose. Proper tension is important. Some stitches, like the feather stitch, are more easily worked vertically. Experiment mixing stitches, colors and weights of thread to get interesting effects.

You may recognize some of these stitches as old friends with other names, just as classic quilt patterns are called by different names depending upon the region of the country or decade you live in. As with quilting, the colors and materials may vary according to your taste or convenience. Heavy thread or yarns work better with heavy fabrics and finer thread with lighter fabrics. Pearl cotton is good for crazy quilts.

Stitches marked with an asterisk (*) are also illustrated on pages 14 and 15. Abbreviations used here include CC1, first contrasting color, and CC2, second contrasting color.

To follow these charts, bring needle up through fabric on odd numbers and down through fabric on even numbers.

Working vertically, make large loop from 1 to 2. Hold loop in place with next loop from 3 to 4. Continue, keeping thread taut but loose enough to curve slightly. Fasten last loop with short straight stitch.

Feather Stitch

Make large cross-stitches,* then add a French knot* above and below each cross.

Cross & Knot

With MC, work line of even herringbone stitches. With CC and straight stitches, stitch "gates" in straight stitches.

Herringbone Gate

With MC, work line of wide herringbone stitches. With CC, use small straight stitches to tie down crossed ends and to work four straight stitches between crossed ends.

Turkey Trot

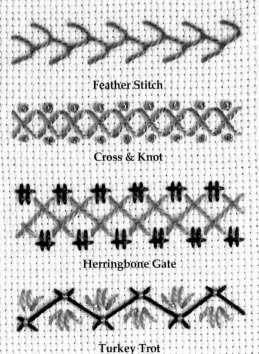

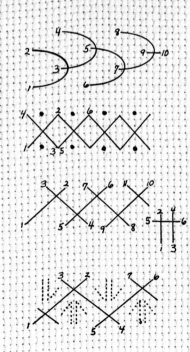

With MC, work "trap": Stitch large loop and tie down with medium straight stitch. Place second loop directly below first loop—chart shows them separated only for clarity. With CC, place a French knot* "fly" in each trap.

Fly Trap

Using CC, work two parallel lines of evenly spaced medium-sized straight stitches. With MC, weave thread under straight stitches, following chart numbers and not piercing the fabric.

Drunken Weaver

Using MC, tie down large loops in zigzag line. Use tiny extra stitch to tie down first and last stitches into "tile" shape. In CC, place "flower" in each "tile," with all down stitches in common center hole.

Flower Tiles

With MC, make groups of two large cross-stitches* separated by a longer straight stitch. Using CC, add groups of three lazy daisy stitches* and French knots* on both sides of chain.

Daisy Chain

In MC, work top row of "tepees" with straight stitches, placing French knot* at top of each tepee. Work bottom row to correspond to top row. With CC, straight stitch center motif inside each pair of tepees.

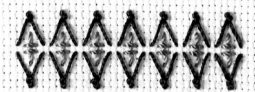

Tepee Town

With MC, work upper line of "bushes" in backstitches, making stitches 2, 4, 8 and 10 all go down same hole. Invert bushes on lower line, placing each bush between two upper bushes. With CC, weave "snake" between both lines of bushes, as shown.

Snake-in-the-Bush

In MC, work groups of three straight stitches in long triangles, alternating direction. In CC, work French knots* at apex of triangles and groups of three straight stitches at base of triangles, with all down stitches through common hole.

Maybelle's Choker

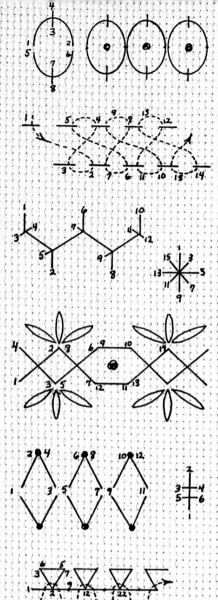
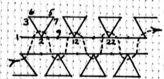
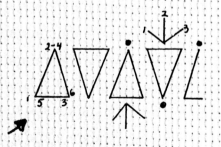

Using MC, work groups of two lazy daisy stitches* and one straight stitch, alternating direction of groups. With CC, place one large French knot* at end of each straight stitch.

Work vertically, making straight stitches in groups of five. All down strokes go into one of two holes, as shown.

Working vertically, make large loop from 1 to 2. Tie down with loop from 3 to 4. Continue, keeping loops in a straight line but alternating direction. Fill in between vertical stitches with groups of three straight stitches that go down in same hole.

With CC, work long and short straight stitches. With MC, weave a line through short stitches; do not pull tightly or pierce fabric.

In MC, work groups of three straight stitches. In CC, weave thread through groups in one direction, then weave back in other direction.

In MC, work a row of herringbone stitches (see Herringbone Gate, page 10). With CC, tie crossed ends with straight stitches.

Use MC and straight stitches to make the "walk." Make "plants" with CC in straight stitches and French knots.*

With MC, work groups of two angled lazy daisy stitches.* Place large French knots* in CC at base of each group.

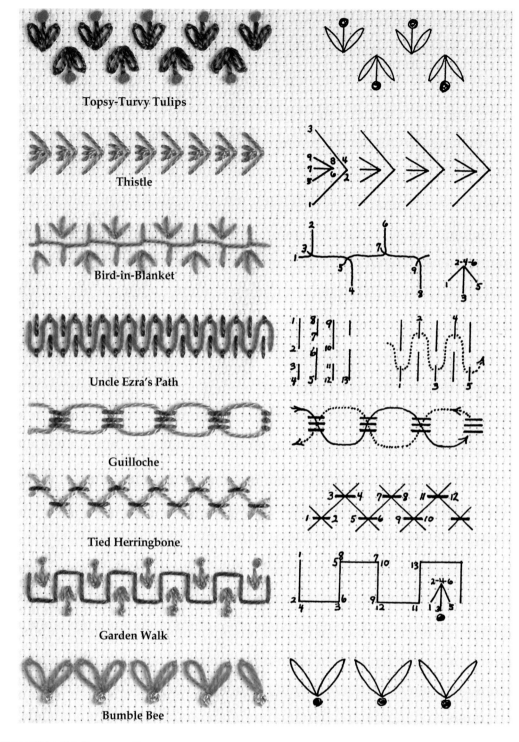

Topsy-Turvy Tulips

Thistle

Bird-in-Blanket

Uncle Ezra's Path

Guilloche

Tied Herringbone

Garden Walk

Bumble Bee

All stitches start at outside edge and go down in center of each "eye." Place eyes with outer edges touching.

In CC, work parallel long straight stitches. In MC, tie down these stitches with short, angled straight stitches. Add a short straight stitch between "dollars."

With MC, make large chain stitch. Make lazy daisy stitches* on each side of chain. With CC, stitch zigzag backstitches between chain and lazy daisies.

Work all in straight stitches. In top of "fan," all stitches start at edge and go down through same center hole. All but one stitch in "handle" go down in same hole close to fan. Invert every other fan.

With MC, work row of parallel graduated straight stitches (mosaic stitch). With CC, work groups of three straight stitches above and below mosaic.

With CC1, work large straight crosses. Using CC2, work standard crosses over straight crosses. With MC, work medium crosses over first and second crosses. Add small crosses between each group.

In MC, work row of even herringbone (see Herringbone Gate, page 10). Using CC1, work another row of herringbone between stitches of first row. With CC2 and straight stitches, tie down center crosses.

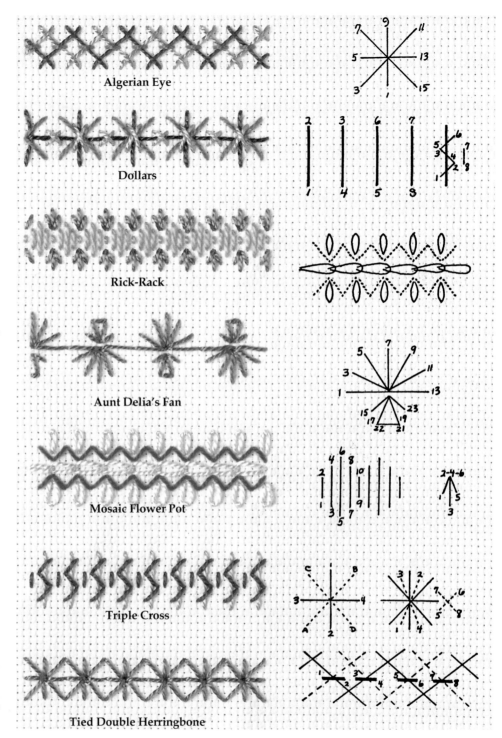

Algerian Eye

Dollars

Rick-Rack

Aunt Delia's Fan

Mosaic Flower Pot

Triple Cross

Tied Double Herringbone

Basic Embroidery Stitches

Slip-Stitch

Alternate tiny stitches from one folded edge to another to make an invisible join. Use slip-stitch to piece fabric scraps together, or to close openings for turning and stuffing.

Quilting or Running Stitch

Weave the needle in and out of the fabric several times, and pull through, keeping the stitches small and even. This is used in quilting and hand sewing.

Stem Stitch

Insert needle from right to left, bringing it out at point where the last stitch went in. Keep the thread below the needle.

Four-Sided Stitch

Form a square by gathering three threads together on each of the square's four sides.

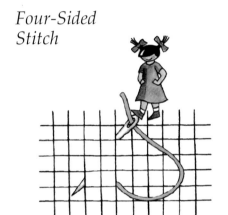

1. Bring needle up through fabric at one corner of a square. Make a straight stitch along one side of square and bring needle up and out at the corner diagonally opposite.

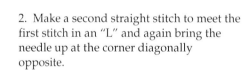

2. Make a second straight stitch to meet the first stitch in an "L" and again bring the needle up at the corner diagonally opposite.

3. Make a third straight stitch to meet the first stitch in a "U" and bring the needle out at the corner diagonally opposite.

4. The last stitch of the first square is the first stitch of the second square. Pull each stitch firmly.

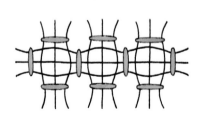

5. Finished four-sided stitches (also known as drawn-thread stitches).

Cross-Stitch

Always work the cross-stitch on an even-weave fabric, such as Aida cloth or home-spun. Unless pattern indicates otherwise, embroider over two-by-two threads. Bring the needle up through the fabric at base of the "X"; work from either left to right or right to left, whichever is more comfortable for you, and work the bottom row of stitches. Insert the needle vertically. Come back across the row and embroider the top half of the "X." All bottom stitches should lie in one direction throughout.

Split Stitch

1. Make a stitch. Bring needle up through fabric, piercing the center of the previous stitch.

2. Insert the needle down through the fabric, half a stitch length beyond the last pierced stitch. The split stitch resembles a delicate chain stitch and makes a fine outline stitch.

French Knot

1. Bring the needle up through the fabric to start the stitch. Wind the thread around the needle once or twice.

Satin Stitch

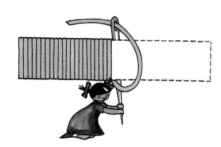

Insert the needle at a slight angle to make vertical stitches that will wrap around the threads of the fabric. You can use the satin stitch for both surface embroidery and drawn-thread work.

Blanket Stitch

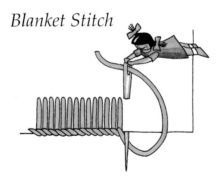

Draw needle up through fabric close to the edge. Working from left to right, insert needle into the fabric and bring it out at the edge, making a loop below the needle. Draw the loop tightly with the emerging thread over the top of it. Maintain an even tension in the stitches to keep the edge flat. (This is also known as a buttonhole stitch.)

French Knot (continued)

2. Insert needle down through the fabric close to the starting stitch. For a bolder effect, try doubling the thread.

Backstitch

Bring needle up through the fabric; insert it to the right, a stitch length back. Bring the needle back out at the left, a stitch length ahead of the work. Keep stitches even. Use backstitch for hand sewing, embroidery and in cross-stitch embroidery to define outlines and contours.

Lazy Daisy Stitch

Bring the needle up through the fabric and reinsert it close to the same spot, forming the thread into a loop. Pull the loop to the desired length, holding it in place with your finger. Then anchor the loop at the bottom with a small straight stitch. Lazy daisy stitches can be used alone or in groups for varying effects.

Needlepoint

Use strands of yarn no longer than 18 inches. Repeatedly pulling a longer length through the canvas will fray and break it. The design area may be worked first and the background filled in later. If you are working from a chart, it will be easier to work the needlepoint row by row, however.

Begin a new yarn by making a knot. Leaving knot on right side, run yarn down through canvas about 1 inch from where you want to begin. Bring needle up at starting point. After the stitches worked later cover the loose end of yarn, clip off the knot. When ending a length of yarn, run it back under a few stitches on wrong side of work.

Gobelin Stitch

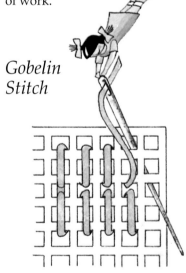

This is a straight stitch that is worked over anywhere from one to six mesh (threads) at a time. Gobelin stitch is used in Bargello and is also a fast way to do borders and backgrounds. Insert needle at bottom of stitch, bring needle straight up over desired number of mesh, then down through canvas making a straight stitch, either vertically or horizontally. Bring needle up through canvas next to first stitch, working from left to right. When this row of stitches is completed, turn work upside down so the next row can be worked from left to right.

Half cross-stitch, continental stitch and basketweave stitch all look the same finished. Basketweave stitch uses more yarn but causes less distortion, making the finished work easier to block and frame.

Continental Stitch

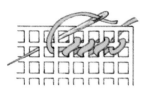

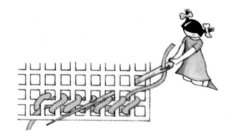

Work a horizontal row completely across from right to left, then turn the canvas upside down, and work back across.

Basketweave Stitch

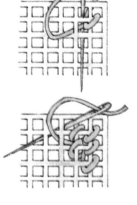

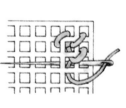

Work diagonally up and down; the stitches on the back of the canvas form a woven pattern.

Half Cross-Stitch

The simplest of all needlepoint stitches is the half cross-stitch, which is always worked from left to right. Start at the bottom of a stitch. Cross over 1 mesh of the canvas (diagonally) and insert needle down and through for next stitch. The needle is always inserted vertically. When the row of stitches is completed, turn work upside down so the next row can be worked from left to right.

Cross-Stitch

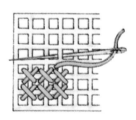

When a slightly more textured effect is desired, cross-stitch is often used for needlepoint. In working designs, each cross-stitch is completed individually. On backgrounds, however, a row of half cross-stitch is completed, then the second half of the stitch is completed on the return. In either case, the stitches must all cross in the same direction.

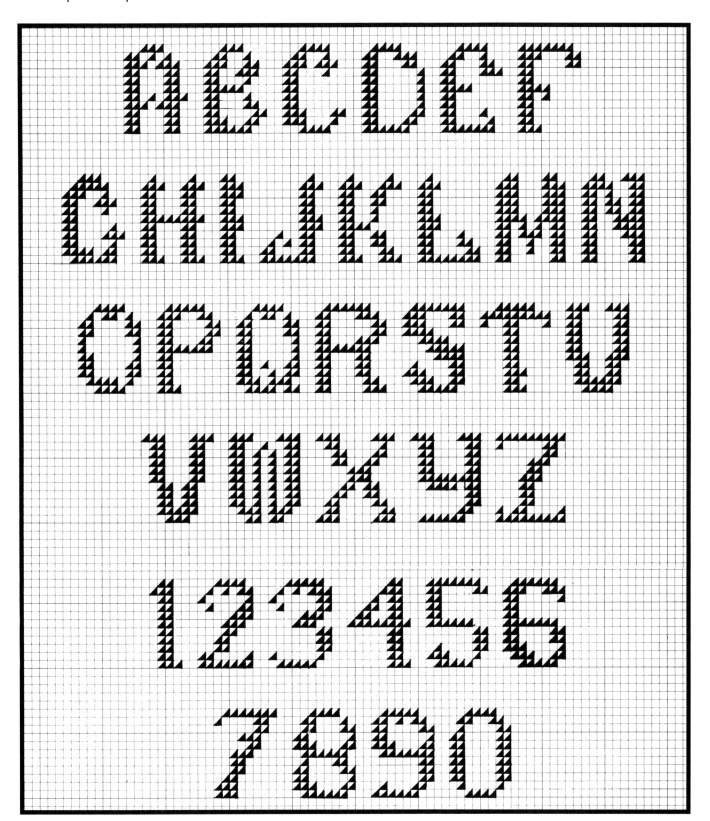

Counted Cross-Stitch Techniques

The linen used in antique samplers turns quite dark with age, a process which is accelerated with exposure to light. You may want to use the following dye recipes to replicate the darkened color of an old sampler. The tea dye will darken the fabric to an off-white; the coffee dye will make a darker, warmer beige color. However, different types of fabric will dye differently, so you may want to dye a test piece first.

Tea: In a kettle, boil enough water to half fill a large pan (a broiling pan, about 8½ by 13 inches works well). While the water is coming to a boil, put five or six bags of ordinary breakfast tea into the pot. Pour in the boiling water and allow it to steep for about 10 minutes. Wring out the tea bags into the water and discard them. Moisten the linen with plain water. Immerse it in the tea bath for 10 minutes and check the color for a match, allowing for the fact that it will dry one shade lighter. Add 1 teaspoon of alum (which you can buy in a drugstore) and stir well before removing the fabric. Alum will set the color so it won't streak if you wash it later. Immerse the linen up to 10 minutes longer if necessary to achieve the desired color. Save the bath and re-immerse the linen if it needs to be darker, but add new alum to the bath.

Coffee: Prepare approximately 6 cups of breakfast coffee. Wet the linen in plain water if you want the dye to take evenly. (If you immerse dry linen in the dye bath, it will color unevenly, as some old samplers have.) Immerse the linen in the coffee and proceed as described for tea.

All samplers are stitched on linen. The number of threads per inch woven into the linen vertically (the warp) and horizontally (the woof) varies. Look for the *design size* (the width and height your stitching will cover). Allow a 3-inch margin on all sides of the design size so the finished sampler can be framed properly.

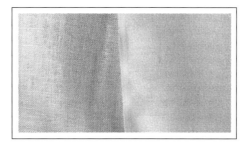

Compare the 25-count linen on the left, woven with 25 threads in each inch, with the 44-count linen on the right. The extra space between every second vertical thread is visible in the more loosely woven linen.

When copying a charted design, purchase linen with the specified thread count if you want your finished piece to be the same size as the original. If you use linen with a different thread count —you may find a more open weave easier to see and count, for example— you can calculate a new design size by counting the number of stitches in the width and the height of the chart. Each square in the chart equals one stitch. Normally, one stitch is taken over two threads (though often over only one thread in parts of some samplers), so divide the number of squares in each dimension of the chart by the thread count (number of threads to the inch) in the same dimension of the linen you buy. Divide the answer in *half* to get

your new design size in inches because most of your stitches will be over *two* threads.

The instructions for some samplers require that you make contemporary even-weave linen replicate the exact counts of the old uneven-weave linen on which the original was stitched. The instructions specify the number of threads to remove from each inch of even weave. Work down (sometimes across) the center of the linen. Slide your needle under each thread before you snip it so you will not cut the adjacent threads. Pull each half of the snipped thread almost to the edge of the linen on each side. Leave the last ½-inch of thread in the linen. Secure them there by backstitching each thread for a few stitches. Then trim the fringe and hand or machine-stitch along the edge depending on whether the edge will show when framed.

To prevent the edges of the linen from fraying, pull long strands from scraps of linen to whipstitch or hem the piece. Work the sampler before you hem your finished work.

Thread: Unless otherwise indicated, work all stitches with two strands of thread. The chart key and instructions indicate when to use one strand or more than two strands of thread. The brands and colors of floss, or silk threads, are also given in the chart or instructions. If the specified thread is not available, substitute the best color match from another manufacturer.

Starting Point: Antique samplers were usually worked from the top down and the outer borders worked before the areas inside them. To locate your starting point, measure down 3 inches from the top and 3 inches in from the left edge (or right edge if you prefer to start your work on the right side and work to the left). Start your first cross next to the nearest vertical thread, as shown opposite.

Bring the needle's point up from the back of the fabric at X. Count up two threads, and over two threads to the right. Go down at O. As you work you will see that you are using the wider opening for each stitch.

Linen woven by machine today has a larger opening between the linen threads every second thread. (This regular variation is more visible in looser weaves such as 25- to 35-count.) If you make your first stitch next to the vertical thread with the larger opening, it will be much easier to count your stitches.

Threading: There are two ways to anchor the first stitch: tying a waste knot (the method used by the children who stitched the original samplers in this collection), and the loop method, which is somewhat quicker, though less durable.

To create a waste knot, tie a simple half-knot (like the first knot you tie before you make the bow in your

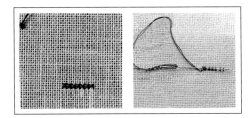

When the length of thread has been used up, snip the waste knot. Rethread the needle with the tail on the back and secure it in the adjacent stitches.

shoelaces) at the very end of the thread. Approximately ½ inch from the spot where you will make your first stitch, pass the needle through from the front of the linen and draw the knot snugly on top. Then start working your stitches. When you run out of thread, snip off the waste knot, being careful not to snip the linen. Turn the linen over and run the needle under the first three stitches on the back. Thread your needle with the loose "tail" of thread hanging down where you snipped off the waste knot. Bury the tail so the first stitch will not pull loose later.

You may use the loop method if you are working with two or any other even number of strands of thread. Fold the length of thread in half and thread the eye of your needle with the two ends together, leaving a loop at the other end. Come up from the back of the linen and do the first half-cross. When you pass the needle through to the back, run it through the loop before coming up for the next half-cross. Tug slightly to secure the thread in the loop.

Reading a Chart: Each stitch shown on the chart is marked by a symbol. The symbol changes to indicate a different color thread and, sometimes, a different number of strands of thread. The chart key in the instructions for each sampler

is a legend for the symbols used in the chart. It gives the color number for the brand of thread used. The instructions and sometimes its chart key explain which stitch to use in each area.

Over-Ones: When you follow the chart to work in cross-stitch, you normally assume that one square on the graph represents one stitch taken over two threads in the linen. However, portions of antique samplers were worked with smaller stitches called over-ones. To work over-ones, work the cross-stitch in the normal way but cross each stitch over only one linen thread instead of the usual two threads. The chart will indicate two to four tiny individual crosses inside one square ⊠ ⊠⊠ or will fill in the portion of the square to be stitched over one thread ◧ ◳ .

Ending and Moving: When you have finished an area and wish to start stitching again in another area of the linen that is further away than the equivalent of three stitches (six linen threads), tie off your strands by running them through the backs of several stitches so no loose end shows. When the chart indicates that you should leave a loose thread, as the children often did in the originals, it is easiest to put them in later with small pieces of leftover threads. Secure them first to the back of another stitch with a knot and then pull them through so they cannot be pulled out accidentally.

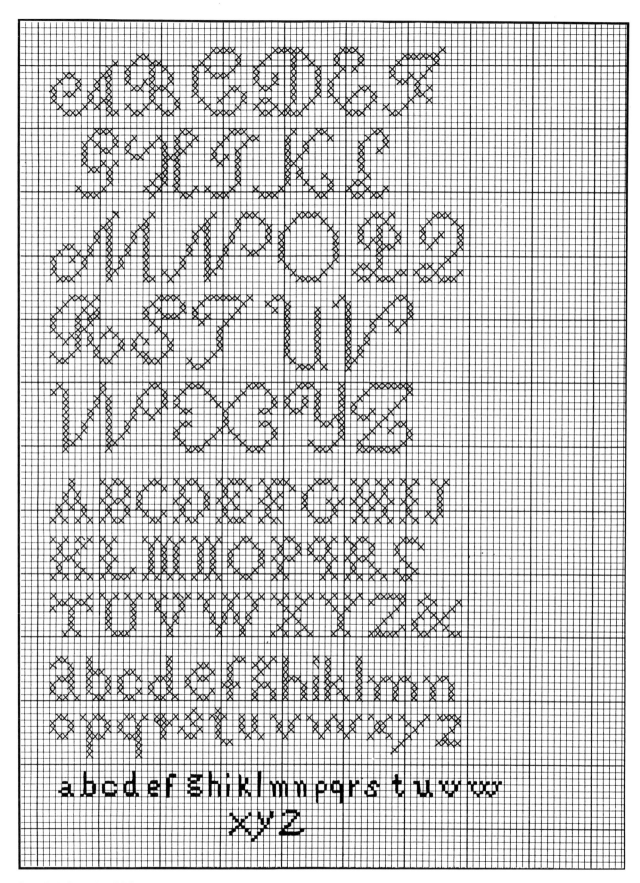

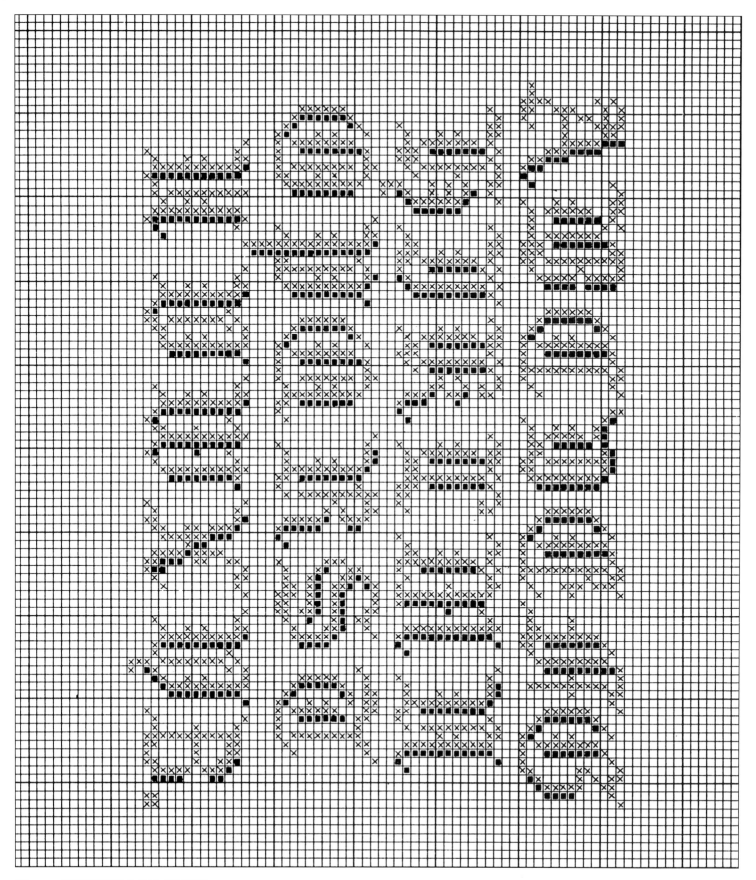

Blocking & Framing Embroidery

Your local needlework shop can block and frame your work, but it's really not difficult to do it yourself.

If you frame your work using laminated foam board, you will not need to block it first unless it is skewed completely out of shape.

Blocking

Clean towel
Tape
Heavy paper the size of the work
Wood board 1" larger than the work
Pencil
Rustproof push-pins or thumbtacks

1. With the piece still in the embroidery frame, wet a clean cloth and lay it on the right side of the needlework. Remove the cloth when dry. If canvas was used and work is unframed, dampen the needlework in cold water and roll in a clean towel.

2. Tape a piece of heavy paper on a large wood board and draw a rectangle the exact outside size your work should be.

3. While the work is still damp (but not dripping) fasten it to the board at each corner and then at center of each side with rustproof push-pins or thumbtacks, making it fit the shape you outlined on the heavy paper.

4. Continue adding pins halfway between those already in place until you have placed pins no more than ½ inch apart all around the piece. Allow the piece to dry completely.

Framing

Traditionally, needlework is framed without glass covering it. This allows the natural fabric to breathe and prevents mildew stains that occur when water from the air condenses inside the glass. However, it will need to be dusted or lightly vacuumed more frequently if you don't use glass!

Picture frame with mounting hardware
Utility knife
Mat board or laminated foam board, ¼" thick, cut ⅛" smaller than interior dimensions of frame
Scissors
Thumbtacks or push-pins
Needle and strong thread or stapler and light-duty staples
Glass (optional)
Tack hammer and small finishing nails (optional)
Brown paper
White glue
Straightedge

1. Remove any hardware from the back of your picture frame.

2. Cut a piece of mat board or foam board with dimensions ⅛ inch smaller than the opening of your picture frame.

3. **If you use mat board**, center the sampler on the white side of the mat board and draw the excess fabric over it. If more than 1½ to 2 inches of extra fabric remains, trim it off. Fasten the fabric to the edges of the board with thumbtacks or push-pins; make sure the threads of the background fabric line up squarely with the edges of the board.

If you use foam board, center your work on the piece you have cut to the appropriate size, folding excess fabric over the edges. Do not trim excess fabric yet. Attach the sampler to the board by inserting push-pins into the sides of the board, into the foam part, all the way around the piece. To get your sampler lined up well on the board, lay your picture frame on top of your board while all the push-pins are still in, and see how straight your lines are. If you need to adjust your fabric, just remove the necessary push-pins, move your fabric and replace the push-pins.

Once you are happy with how well your needlework is lined up, let it sit with the pins in it for about an hour or so before you lace or staple it. Often the fabric will give a little more under the stress of the pins, even if it has been blocked.

4. **If you use mat board**, fold and miter the corners under, then stitch the edges together with strong thread. Lace the edges of the fabric together horizontally and vertically across the back of the frame with long strands of strong thread. Remove tacks or pins.

If you use foam board, fold excess fabric to the back of the board. Using a stapler with light-duty staples, staple the excess fabric about 2 inches from the edge on the back of the board, all the way around the piece. Do corners last, simply folding them down and stapling them. Remove push-pins. Trim any excess fabric about 2 inches from the staples.

5. If you wish to use glass, clean it now and insert it in the frame.

Before you put your needlework into its frame, wrap a piece of masking tape, sticky-side down, around your fingers and brush it all over your sampler. This will remove those tiny pieces of lint that try to escape your eyes until the piece is all assembled in its frame.

6. Put the picture in the frame face down. Attach it using the hardware that came with the frame; or, carefully hammer small finishing nails into the center of each side of the rabbet, and then every 3 or 4 inches around the inside of the frame.

7. To protect the back of the needlework, cut a sheet of brown paper (an old grocery bag works beautifully) several inches larger than the entire back. Remove any hanging hardware attached to back of frame. Rub white glue on the back of your picture frame, then place the brown paper on top so that it overhangs on each edge. With a straightedge as a guide and using the utility knife, trim the paper to size— about ¹⁄₁₆ inch from the edge of the frame—while the glue is still wet. Attach hanging hardware to the back of the frame.

Antique Cross-Stitch Motifs & Borders

In early America, girls learned to cook by helping in the kitchen, and to stitch and recognize their letters by creating samplers. A 9-year-old named Charlotte Frobisher stitched the one shown above in 1805. We worked exact replicas of cross-stitch motifs from authentic schoolgirl samplers onto rounds of linen fabric large enough to cover tops of jars filled with home-made preserves. The motifs are (clockwise from upper right) *Esther's Basket*, *Repeating Rose*, *Pennsylvania Dutch* and *Quilt Star* (from Charlotte's sampler). The jar covers work up quickly and can be used again when jars are empty.

Charts with accompanying DMC color and symbol guides for each of the four motifs are on the pattern page. See page 15 for instructions to work the basic cross-stitch. You may work your designs in an embroidery hoop or hold the project in your hand, as you prefer. If you want to work with a hoop, a 4- or 5-inch one works well for these small pieces.

For all motifs:
6" square of either Hardanger fabric or Aida cloth as described
Straight pin
DMC embroidery floss in colors listed
No. 26 tapestry needle
Embroidery hoop (optional)
3" circle of double-sided self-adhesive board
Fabric glue
Scissors
Mason or Ball canning jar with a 3" lid

1. Fold fabric in half, then in half again to find center; mark the center with a straight pin. Arrows on the charts indicate the center of each design.
2. Begin cross-stitching in center of fabric with color and number of strands of floss indicated, using the tapestry needle.
3. After finishing the cross-stitch, apply the fabric to the jar lid: Center, and then stick the fabric to a 3-inch-diameter circle of self-adhesive board, available in crafts and needlework shops. Trim the fabric to fit the board and apply fabric glue to the edges to prevent fraying.

To make a puffy jar lid, insert a 2-inch circle of quilt batting to the center of the self-adhesive board before attaching the fabric.

4. Expose the adhesive on the other side of the board and press the jar lid into the adhesive. Screw the jar top over the fabric.

Quilt Star
Design size: 15 by 15 stitches

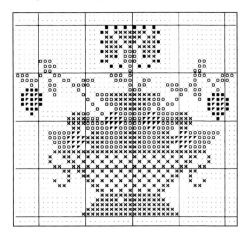

The Quilt Star motif is taken from a reproduction of Charlotte Frobisher's sampler, partially shown in the photo opposite. The original sampler is at the Essex Institute of Salem, Massachusetts. Stitch Charlotte's motif on either 22-count ivory Hardanger fabric over two threads, as we did, or on 11-count ivory Aida cloth over one thread. Work with two or three strands of floss, whichever you prefer.

Esther's Basket
Design size: 40 by 44 stitches

Esther Elizabeth Histed of North Erie County, Pennsylvania, began a sampler in 1833, when she was 11 years old. She died before her work was complete. This motif is from her unfinished sampler, which is held by the Museum of Fine Arts, Boston. Work Esther's Basket over one thread of 22-count ivory Hardanger fabric, using one strand of floss.

Pennsylvania Dutch
Design size: 28 by 50 stitches

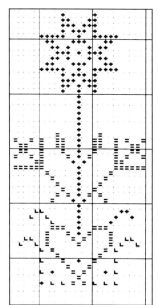

This heart-basket design is from a "show" towel worked by Susana Bartholomew in 1824, when she was about 9 years old. These towels were stitched by Pennsylvania Dutch girls for their trousseaux. They were used by young homemakers to cover up ordinary kitchen towels when company came to call. Susana's towel sampler, which measures 40 inches in length, is part of the collection of the Quakertown Historical Society in Quakertown, Pennsylvania. Work the Pennsylvania Dutch motif over one thread of 22-count ivory Hardanger fabric, using one strand of floss.

Repeating Rose
Design size: 7 by 10 stitches, each motif

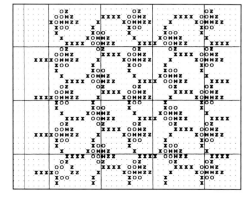

Mary E. Carpenter of Rochester, New York, stitched a sampler while at school in 1829, at age 10. This pattern is from a border on Mary's sampler, which is held by the Margaret Woodbury Strong Museum in Rochester. Work the Repeating Rose pattern on 14-count ivory Aida cloth, using two strands of floss. Work the entire design as shown, and allow the jar lid to cover the outermost stitches.

DMC	Symbol	Color			
833	◩	gold	518	Ⓣ	bright blue
3371	◼	dark brown	727	Ⓤ	yellow
407	☒	rose	3350	⊞	dark pink
992	Ⓞ	green	930	⊟	dark blue
350	⊡	red	951	Ⓩ	lightest rose
962	Ⓛ	light pink	3064	Ⓗ	dark rose
			612	⊠	beige

Until the turn of this century most young girls learned decorative embroidery at the same age as they learned their ABC's. When European families arrived in America, the women often brought with them a stitched record of the designs and borders they favored.

The work shown on pages 26 through 29 was stitched by a 6-year-old English child named Sarah, who, as an adult, brought it to America sometime in the mid-19th century. In those days, the work was done only on linen, and then, as now, motifs like these worked in simple cross-stitch could find many homes: a floral on an apron, a heart on a shirt pocket, a classic geometric around the edge of a collar or the hem of a dress, a cat on a bib, a tree and a bird as ecological motifs on a toddler's romper. The opportunities are endless, the work personal and unique, the designs as old as time.

All these motifs are simple cross-stitch worked on linen over two threads. See page 15 to learn the basic cross-stitch.

The thread is DMC Flower Thread. One strand of thread was used on 32-count ivory linen.

This 32-count linen has 16 threads per inch. Flower Thread, which looks like cotton, is worked with one strand because it is thicker than floss.

The soft, faded colors of the Flower Thread tend to make these motifs appear antique. In the 17th and 18th centuries, however, most decorative embroidery was not worked with cotton thread, which has a matte finish like Flower Thread, but rather with silk thread, which has a sheen more like modern floss. We've provided the DMC color codes below for both Flower Thread and floss so you may choose the appropriate thread for your piece—depending on whether you prefer an antique look with a cottonlike finish or an authentic look with a silky sheen.

Use a no. 24 tapestry needle for either linen or Aida cloth.

DMC Color Codes	
Flower Thread	Floss
O = 2503	O = 503
X = 2823	X = 924
E = 2950	E = 950
I = 2644	I = 613

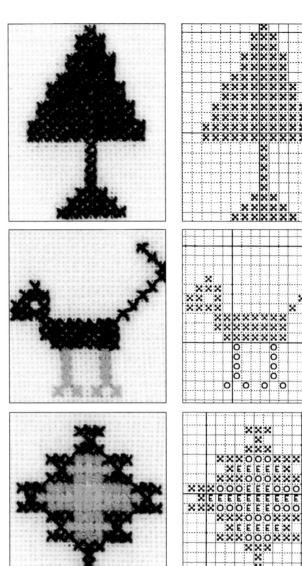

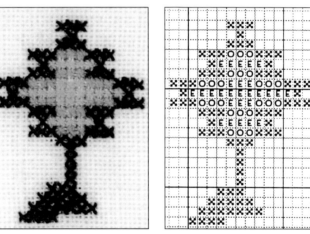

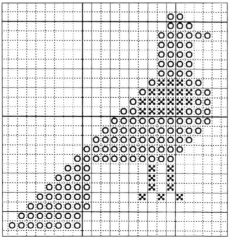

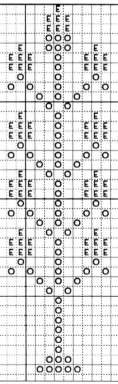

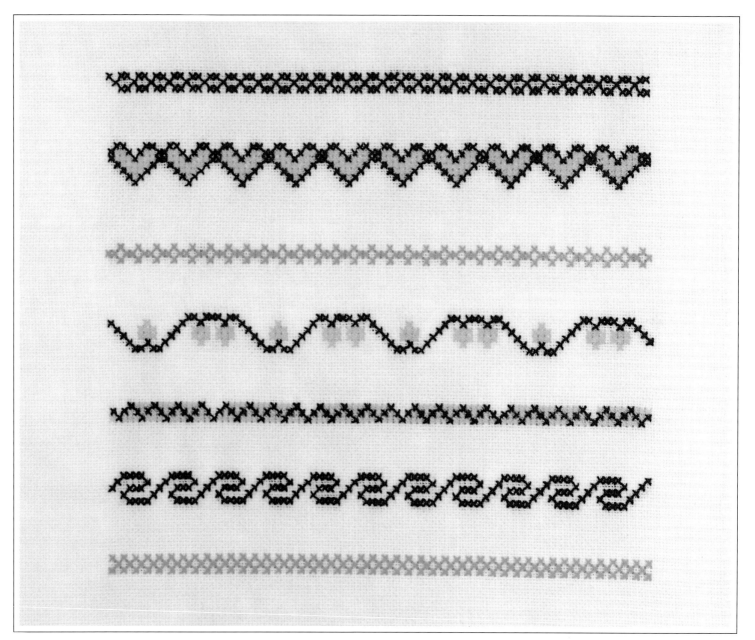

Embroidered motifs have been around since ancient times. The oldest surviving piece of embroidery is Peruvian, from the years A.D. 400 to 500. Its many human, animal, bird and mythological motifs look curiously contemporary today.

Linen has traditionally been the fabric of preference. Scraps bearing motifs and initials found in Egyptian tombs may have been the forerunners of our monogrammed towels and shirts. It took a great deal of time to grow, spin and weave linen fabric by hand, and the items made from it often looked similar, so it was important to put initials on every article, even undergarments, in the household inventory.

The type of embroidery on clothing often was an indication of the wearer's social rank. In the Roman Empire, it was a design worked with purple thread; in Imperial China, a crane motif; (an alligator in yuppie America?). In Medieval Europe, members of the embroiderers' guild (a trade union of only the most skilled masters) produced some of the world's most beautiful needlework. Interestingly, in Britain at that time, all master embroiderers were men.

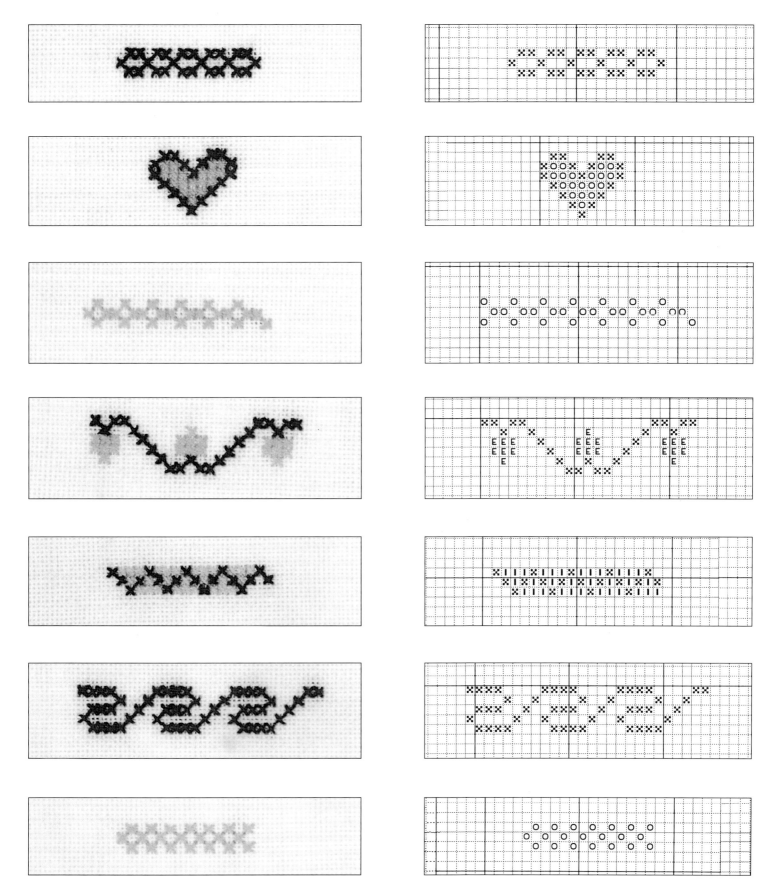

Crazy-Quilt Stitchery

This circa 1840 sampler quilt is a masterful blend of traditional quilt patterns and 19th-century fashionable crazy-quilt ingredients: scraps of lush velvets and rich satins, embellished with creative stitchery and appliqué. The result is a lasting personal statement, full of originality and fun. Isn't that what quilting and needle-work are all about? Since traditional crazy quilts were usually made of individual squares, it's easy to play with these techniques on a smaller project like a crib quilt, wall hanging or pillow. Use this photo and those on pages 31 and 33 for inspiration. Or piece your scraps randomly, in the typically "crazy" manner.

A crazy quilt is a family history, made of bits and scraps of lace and satin from old dresses and gowns, ribbons from fairs attended long ago, lace from long-worn-out tablecloths, silk from ties the wrong color or too spotted to wear.

First, sort fabric by colors, cutting off pieces from large lengths to store away for future quilts. Pull old ties apart and press them flat and cut flat sections from pieces of clothing. Spread the material out on the dining-room table like a palette from which to choose your colors.

A randomly pieced crazy quilt is made of scraps of material that are basted and then embroidered onto 14-inch muslin squares. Finished squares are then stitched together into a quilt. An old sheet or two will provide ample backing squares.

Piecing "Crazy" Squares

1. Start with several patterned silk scraps and lay them randomly on the muslin backing. Lay other pieces between them to completely cover the muslin. Remember to have plenty of overlap so the edges of each piece can be turned under.

2. View each square as a separate composition, like a painting: The harmonious colors, contrasting textures and variety of sizes in the pieces of fabric you choose are important elements. Once the square is laid out, pin each piece loosely in the center and begin turning under edges. There should be no raw edges within a square. Turn the edges at the ironing board, pressing them under and then pinning the pieces in place on the muslin as they are done. The outer edges of each square can be left raw,

Appliqués, like the leaf above, add to the fun of a crazy quilt. They are often symbolic, telling something about the maker or the recipient of a gift quilt. Note that the structure of the leaf has been embossed onto the velvet by pressing them together.

Along with the necessary border embroidery, Victorian quilts also have embroidered pictures in the plain squares.

since they will be covered when the blocks are sewn together into the quilt. Heavy fabrics like velvet that are hard to turn are "bottom pieces," whose raw edges will be overlaid by surrounding patches of thinner fabrics.

3. When the pieces are pressed and pinned, baste each edge to hold the turned edges in place. Remove pins and press the entire square. It should lie perfectly flat. If it does not, unbaste and redo it to remove the pucker.

4. The embroidery is stitched freehand and can be as plain or as fancy as you choose. Each square should have as many different stitches as possible. Victorians judged the elegance of their crazy quilts by the variety and excellence of their workmanship. Almost any embroidery stitch will do: chain, double chain, outline, spaced rows of stem stitches, feather stitch, buttonhole stitch, cross-stitch or even rows of French knots. See pages 10 to 13 for instructions and ideas.

5. Create eye-catching borders just by changing the size or proportion of the common stitches and by using a combination of them, such as a line of stem stitches evenly spaced over a row of cross-stitches of a different color.

6. Basting can be removed once the embroidery is done. If you are making a quilt, the square should then be pressed smooth and packed away flat until the other blocks are completed.

Crazy-Quilt Pillow

Pieced block, 12" square
2 squares, 20" each, of fabric for backing and border (a velvet to match velvet in square works well)
Polyester fiberfill; thread to match fabric
4-ply embroidery floss in desired colors

1. To make the border, cut an 11-inch square out of the center of a 20-inch square. Make ½-inch cuts diagonally into the corners of the "frame" and turn under the ½ inch of velvet on the inside of the frame. Place this over the completed crazy-quilt block and baste in place. Check the measurements to make sure it is square.

2. Using four-ply embroidery floss, run a row of feather stitch over the velvet, close to the edge, making sure your stitches catch all layers of fabric through to the muslin backing. When the embroidery is completed, stitch three sides of the pillow top to the 20-inch square of velvet backing, right sides together, and turn. Press carefully, stuff the pillow and close the opening with very discreet overcast stitches.

Assembling a Quilt

The number of square blocks you will need depends on the size of the quilt and on the method used in joining them together. The traditional crazy quilt was made by putting all the squares together so that the borders of each block melted into the overall jumble. This method takes 63 squares for a double-bed quilt that is 9 by 7 feet.

Another common style of assembly which shows off the squares with more elegance involves placing 3-inch strips of dark velvet between the squares, so that each is framed and separate. Six rows of seven 12-inch squares, each separated by velvet, or a total of 42 squares are needed. These long rows are then sewn to velvet strips the length of the quilt. The velvet strips should be cut 4½ inches wide to allow generous ¾-inch seams on each side. The entire quilt is then bordered with a 4-inch band of velvet, mitered at each corner.

As the quilt is assembled, the squares must be kept perfectly straight. It is helpful to make a 12-inch-square cardboard template and trace around it with a pencil on the muslin side of each block. The pencil line serves as a stitching guide.

Silk and satin crazy quilts were usually tied, not quilted, because quilting would ruin the effect of the embroidery. Stitch three sides of the quilt top to a backing the same size, right sides together. Turn and press the edges lightly. Press velvet face down on a piece of extra velvet to preserve the nap. Close open side with very discreet overcast stitches.

A batted filling can be put in a silk crazy quilt, but it's not a good idea. Since these are usually showpieces, the warmth of quilt batting is unnecessary and the fabric and design are not suited to quilting or washing.

Traditional silks and velvets are both expensive and difficult backing materials to work with. A fine-grained cotton fabric in a color that blends well with the quilt might be a better choice.

After the backing is joined to the quilt top, the entire quilt should be tied, or "tacked." Lay the quilt out perfectly flat on an ironed sheet, using its corners as a guide to keep the quilt corners square. Pin lightly in the seams at the corners between the blocks. Once the blocks are pinned, you can move the quilt to a tabletop.

Make a tack with four-strand embroidery floss in each corner of each block, drawing the thread through and back again, and tying the ends together firmly. Trim the ends to about ¼ inch. Tacking keeps the quilt top in place and keeps it square.

Crib Quilt or Wall Hanging

Piece a small crazy quilt and decorate it with lots of stitchery that tells a visual story about a baby's family history or an older child's hobbies and interests—embroidered field hockey sticks or ballet slippers can be just as interesting as birds and flowers. You'll create an heirloom that will someday be a conversation piece for the recipient's own children and grandchildren. To make it even more meaningful, use scraps of fabric from baby's family or from the child's own outgrown clothing. To make your work a wall hanging, sew a strip of fabric just below the top edge of the quilt back. Make it wide enough to accommodate a length of wooden dowel. Leave the ends open so the dowel will slip through the "sleeve" and be suspended from brackets on the wall.

This 31- by 24½-inch crib quilt, pieced in the traditional style around 1900, is inspiration for a wonderful addition to baby's nursery or a lovely wall hanging for an older child's bedroom. Try to use fabric from your child's outgrown wardrobe.

Hems & Monograms

A monogram on a shirt pocket or bath towel is elegant and practical, but one on a hand-hemmed hankie, cuff or napkin strikes an unmistakable tone of quality and taste. The *A* pictured here is worked in padded satin stitch, which can be applied to any fabric. The *M*, cross-stitched in two shades of floss, and the decorative hems must be worked on linen or other fabric with threads that can be counted. We hemmed 26-count pure ivory linen with a 10-gram ball of no. 12 pearl ecru cotton thread and a no. 26 tapestry needle. See pages 20 to 22 for alphabet charts. For stitches, see pages 14 and 15. Work the *A* monogram in DMC 739 floss following the chart on page 21. Photocopy the letter to the desired size and pin it in place. Using two strands of floss, outline it in running stitch through the paper. Remove the paper without distorting the stitches. Fill in the outline with satin stitches. Change to four strands of floss and satin stitch over that padding, keeping the floss flat. Cross-stitch the *M* monogram with two strands of DMC 926 and 927 floss following the chart on page 22.

Decorative Hemstitching

1. **To Prepare Openwork:** *Count 10 threads in from edge of fabric. Pass needle under the 11th thread and lift up the thread.*

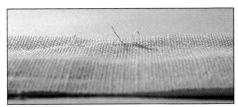

2. *Snip this thread and withdraw it from the entire length of the fabric. Repeat the procedure for the other three sides.*

❧ *The thread will pull out more easily if you pry it up with a needle every few inches and keep pulling it free in stages.*

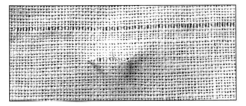

3. *Count 10 more linen threads in toward center of fabric. Snip that thread and remove it as described above. Repeat this procedure for the remaining three sides, leaving an open band around all four sides of the fabric.*

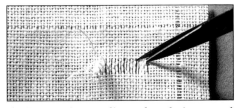

4. *Count 10 more linen threads in toward the center. To prepare the slip-stitched hem, pictured with the* **A** *monogram on the page opposite, snip and withdraw the next five linen threads on all four sides of the fabric.*

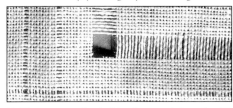

5. *To prepare the ladder hems pictured with the* **M** *monogram, snip and withdraw the next seven threads. Repeat on all four borders. Note that a large square hole opens up in each corner where the open bands meet.*

1. **To Miter Corners and Edges:** *Snip off each corner of the fabric even with the second line of drawn threads as shown by the green stitches in the photo above.*

2. *On the wrong side of the fabric, fold over the snipped corner so that it is even with the outer edge of the open square.*

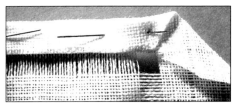

3. *Fold an adjacent edge along the first drawn thread. Fold it again just to the edge of the open area, not into it. Pin or baste the folds and repeat on the other sides.*

1. **To Hem Outer Edge:** *Thread a tapestry needle with #12 pearl cotton or matching floss and knot one end. Start at left end of one fold and bury the knot inside the fold.*

2. *Catch the first two threads in a loop. Pull the needle through and cross over the top of your looping stitch, as you would to start the second cross in a cross-stitch.*

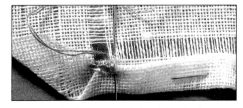

3. *Catch both layers of the folded edge and pull needle through. Continue along outer edges of all four sides. Use buttonhole stitches to bind bottom edges of holes in corners.*

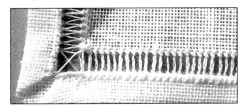

1. **To Hem Inner Edge:** *To make the ladder border shown with the* **M** *monogram, repeat the same stitch along the other side of the openwork on all four sides.*

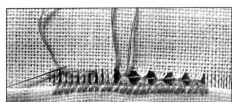

2. *To make the slip-stitched hem shown with the* **A** *monogram, slip the needle under three pairs of threads and bring it around to capture them in a loop, but don't draw it tight.*

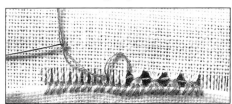

3. *Bring the needle up through the loop and pull the knot, gathering the three pairs of threads together in the center but letting them fan out toward their ends on each side.*

Schoolgirl Sampler

Their naive simplicity and rich colors make cross-stitch sampler motifs as popular today as they were when schoolgirls worked them into their samplers in colonial times. We adapted a sampler stitched by an 11-year-old schoolgirl in 1792. Fanny Mots's original sampler, shown opposite, is now in the permanent collection of the Essex Institute Museum in Salem, Massachusetts. The simplified design shown here is done with dots of color from fabric markers instead of stitches. In place of her name, we substituted a poignant phrase that Early American girls often worked into their samplers. When you transfer this motif onto your apron, shirt, canvas bag or other fabric article, you may substitute your name for this saying or the name of the recipient if you are making a gift. We've provided a pattern for the motif shown here and an extra lowercase alphabet for you to use to personalize your work.

We worked our design with oil-based permanent fabric markers on a separate fabric panel. That way, you can remove the panel before washing the apron if you like. As an option, you can decorate an 8-inch-square pocket, following instructions given here. To sew the pocket in place, turn down and hem the top edge, fold remaining three sides under ½ inch, pin in position and topstitch in place.

1 piece off-white fabric, approximately 10 by 13", prewashed (we used 100% cotton of medium weight and texture)
Masking tape
Fabric markers in desired colors (we used red, olive green, gold, rust, light blue and medium blue)
Ready-made apron in a matching or contrasting fabric
1½ yards off-white gros-grain ribbon, ⅜" wide
Thread to match
Straight pins
Iron, to transfer design on bound-in sheet

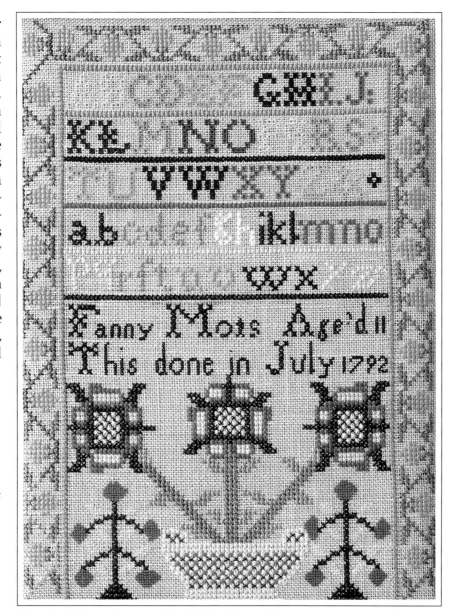

The original sampler created in 1792 by Fanny Mots.

flood with paint. Try to purchase a marker that is close to the fabric color to touch up blots. Applying tiny dots of color, fill in the design on the pattern.

To decorate a pocket that has already been sewn onto your apron, place a piece of cardboard inside the pocket to prevent the markers from bleeding through the pocket onto the skirt.

3. When you have completely colored in the design with dots, follow the pen manufacturer's instructions to set the colors.

4. Zigzag stitch around the sampler panel, about ⅜ inch from the edge of the design. Trim fabric close to the stitching.

5. Pin the sampler panel in place on the apron bib. Baste the panel to the apron, stitching close to the edge of the fabric.

6. Starting near a corner, pin the ribbon in place, covering the basting and panel edges. Make mitered corners by folding as shown below. When you return to the first corner, trim the ribbon at an angle and slip it under the other folded end to complete the mitered look. Pin in place, completely hiding the raw ends of the ribbon. Topstitch ribbon through all layers along both inside and outside edges.

To make this motif in a different size, transfer the design onto plain paper and enlarge or reduce with a photocopier. Tape the photocopy to a light box or sunny window. Tape the fabric on top of it. The light from either source will make the pattern visible through the fabric.

1. Following the directions on the heat transfer pattern (see large, bound-in pattern provided), iron the design onto the fabric panel.

2. The marks on the pattern indicate changes in color from area to area and are not codes for specific colors. Use the photo opposite or the photo of the original sampler here as a general color guide. Since fabric markers come in fewer colors than embroidery floss, you may have to alter the color scheme to accommodate the marker colors available. Practice on a scrap of fabric before starting work. To prevent a marker from leaving blots of color on fabric, check the tip of the marker often; wipe the tip if it has started to

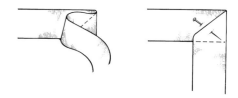

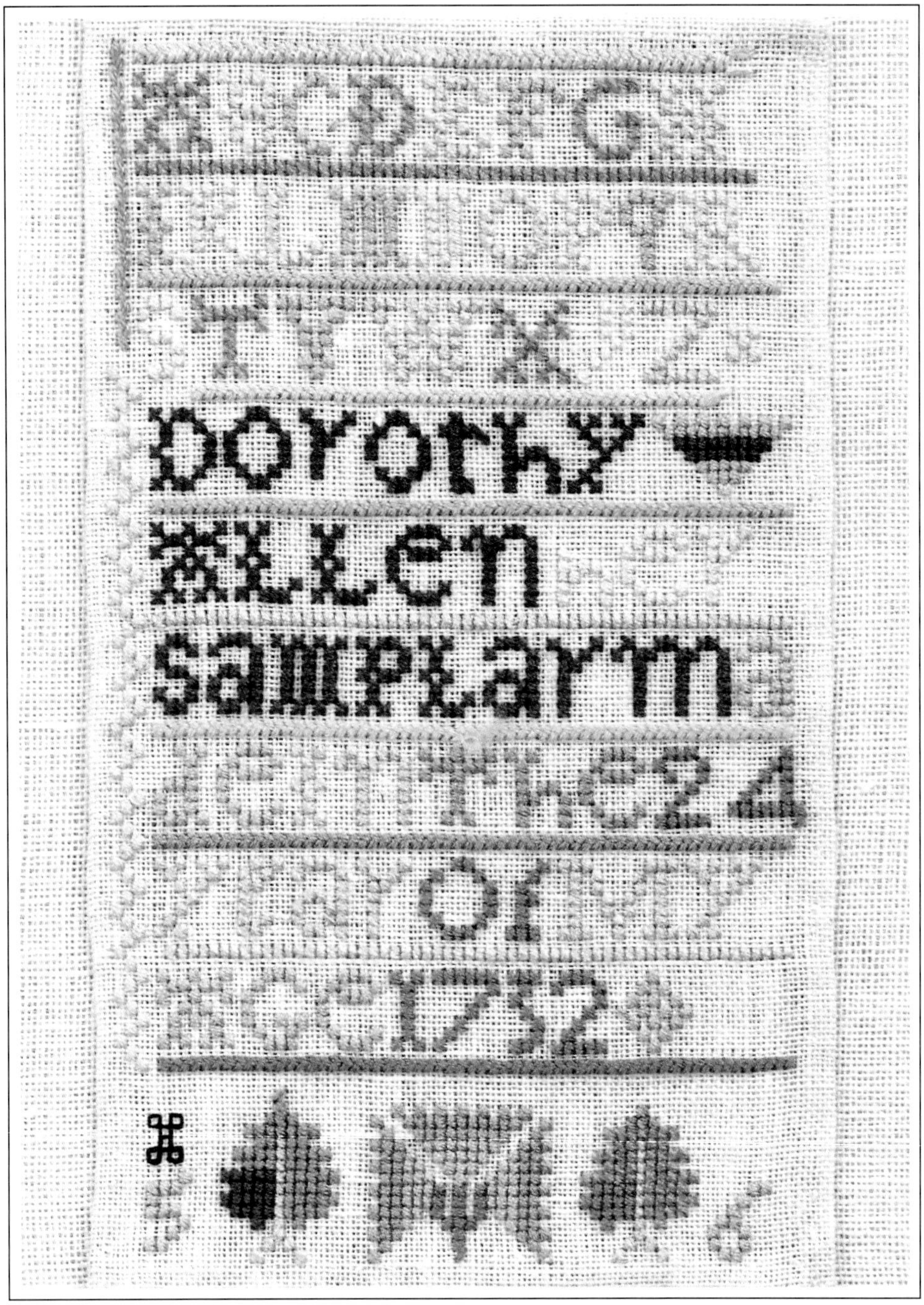

Historic Sampler

The chart and instructions given here will allow you to stitch an exact replica of this antique, cross-stitch sampler on display at the Bennington Museum in Vermont. The genealogical evidence suggests that this very Dorothy Allen was the first cousin of the famous patriot Ethan Allen of "Green Mountain Boys" fame. She finished hers at 24 years old—more than twice the average age of children who worked samplers in her time—a full 45 years before America's war for independence began.

Hers is a band sampler in miniature size. Until the early 18th century, the width that linen could be woven was limited by the width of narrow looms. For that reason, the older samplers, especially English ones, were stitched on relatively long, narrow bands of linen. The original size of the linen on which Dorothy stitched measured 3⅞ by 6½ inches, including ⅛-inch hems on all four sides.

Materials

9⅞ by 12½ inches of 35-count ivory linen; Au Ver a Soie® silk as shown in the Chart Key (note that some stitches are blended); no. 26 tapestry needle.

Directions

Work with one strand of Au Ver a Soie® silk unless otherwise specified. (One strand is equal in thickness to two strands of DMC floss.)

Near the bottom, work the group of boxes that are located over the numeral **5** in four-sided stitch with a single strand of 1425 navy, except for the bottom two boxes, which are worked with two strands.

CHART KEY

SYMBOL	Au Ver a Soie®	COLOR
O	1814	med. dk. green
◤	1745	lt. slate blue
II	1732	gray
Z	4113	rosy brown
L	2231, 2234	lt. gold/gold blend
◥	2223	green-gold
◪	3832	tan
K	3723	green
E	3721	lightest green
ǁ	1714, 1745	blue/slate blue, blend
•	3831	lt. tan, 1 str.
⊕	3426	darkest green
⁙	3836	dk. brown
	1425	navy: 4-sided st.
■	1744	slate blue

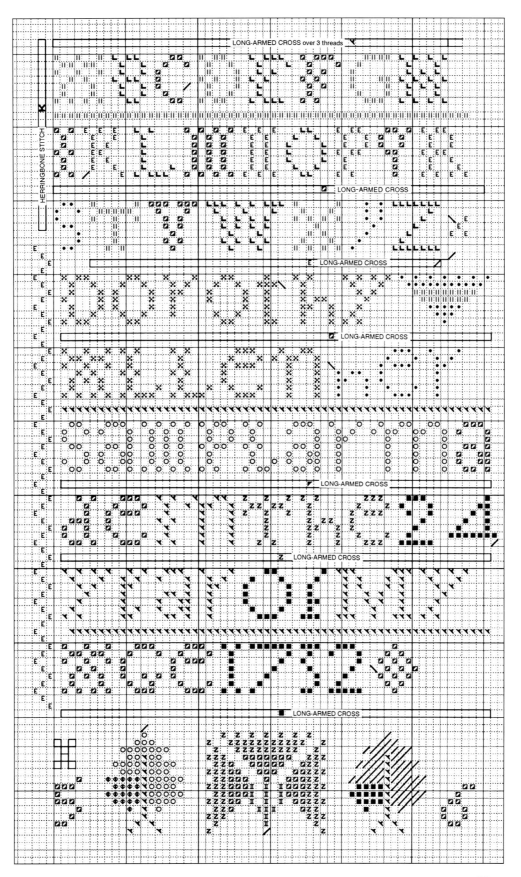

Count threads very carefully as you could ruin the beauty of your sampler if the name and date are off center. Use a piece of graph paper to assist you. If the child's name is very long, eliminate the two sunflower motifs for extra room. Abbreviate the names of long months.

Design Size

119 threads wide by 138 threads high (approximately 8½ by 10 inches on no. 14 fabric; approximately 6⅝ by 7¾ inches on no. 18 fabric). Be sure to allow 6 inches extra for finishing and framing.

Instructions

"Backstitch" is abbreviated as BKST. A single straight line in any direction indicates a BKST, not a color. Start stitching at center of sampler, matching it to center of fabric. All stitches are in two-ply floss unless otherwise noted. See pages 14 and 15 for guidance with stitches; see pages 23 and 46–49 for blocking and framing instructions.

Border

The center of each flower is four BKST in DMC 725 radiating from center of hole, as per chart.

Bunnies

Use two ¾ stitches to form nose. BKST around each completed bunny in one-ply 838 adding a French knot for an eye.

Children

BKST all completed outlines in one-ply 844.

Scandinavian Girl: BKST design on apron in one-ply 356. BKST lacing on vest in 937. Use ¾ stitches to round off tops of puff sleeves. Use 931 for tiny BKST bows near ends of braids.

Dutch Boy: Use ¾ stitches for points on wooden shoes.

American Girl: BKST design on apron in one-ply 844. Place tiny bow in one-ply 221 where pigtails meet head.

Alphabet: Crossed lines in small motif at end of alphabet are BKST in 356. Place your own initials after the motif.

Birth Sampler

Cross-stitch the first letter of each name in color, then backstitch the rest of the name and date. (See the backstitch alphabets shown opposite.) Standard cross-stitch is used throughout except that the flowers at the children's feet are long backstitches topped with French knots. In the border, the centers of the flowers are four tiny backstitches radiating from a center point, which makes them more realistic than a simple cross-stitch would. Chart and DMC colors are shown opposite.

Name and Date: Use whichever alphabet you prefer (see pages 20 to 22 for alphabets), using cross-stitches for capital letters in color. BKST other letters and date, using a smaller alphabet, in 844.

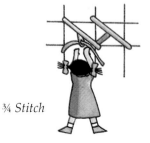

¾ Stitch

Color Key
(One skein each)

Symbol		Color
·		White
/		951
∴		422
⊙		223
∨		221
≻		554
h		932
6		931
+		725
Φ		783
요		471
✕		469
S		937
●		356
∧		842
C		841
✳		838
✦		433
⊕		844
■		Black

Stitch in the middle of the sampler the name and birth date of the infant you wish to commemorate. The color legend (above left) shows the graphic symbol used in the chart to designate each color, a photo of the color floss and its DMC number shown in the instructions on page 40.

Mottoes from Antique Samplers

Mottoes found on the earliest American samplers tend to be brief, stating the child's name, age and the date the sampler was completed. The most common rhymes were "When this you see, remember me" and "[Name, Name] is my name and with my nedle [needle]

I did [wrought] the same." Like these simple epigrams, few verses stitched into samplers in the 18th and early 19th centuries were original. Most were copied from sermons, scripture or other samplers and appear to have been lessons in humility as well as stitchery.

Caty Langdon is my name/And with my needle I rought the same/And if my skil had been better/I would have mended every letter. (1630)

Eunice Pettengil is my/name & with my ha/nds I wrought the/Same Steal Not Th/is For Fear OF/SHAME FOR Here You/Read The Owners/Name. I Wrought/This in The Year 17/91 Being In The 11T/H Year OF My Age/& WAS Born OCT 28/WN M [West Newton, Massachusetts] (1791)

Francis & Sarah Knowles My parents Dear/Paid for this which I have heare (1732)

Mary Ann Lucy Gries is my name/ Marietta is my station Heaven/is my dwelling place and/Christ is my salvation when I/am dead and in my grave and/all my bones are rotten/when this you see Remember me/else I shall be forgotten. (1826)

In prosperity friends are plenty In Adversity not one in twenty (1684)

Defer not til tomorrow to be wise/ Tomorrow s sun to thee may never rise (1802)

A blind woman's soliloquy./Are not the sparrows daily fed by thee,/And wilt thou clothe the lillies and not me./ Begone distrust! I shall have clothes and bread,/While lillies flourish, and the birds are fed. (Martha Perry c 1800)

My friends I hope you are pleased & so shall I/If this my work I may get credit by/ Much Labor & much time it hath me cost/I will take care that none of it be lost. (1767)

No Star so bright/As my delight. (1792)

Sarah Ann Souder worked this in great/ speed And left it here for you to read (c 1775)

Adam alone in Paradise did grieve,/ And thought Eden a desert without Eve,/Until God pitying of his lonesome state/Crowned all his wishes with a loving mate./What reason then hath Man to slight or flout her,/That could not live in Paradise without her? (1796)

While hostile foes our coasts invade,/In all the pomp of war arrayed,/American be not dismayed,/Nor fear the Sword or Gun./While innocence is all our pride,/ And virtue is our only Guide/Women would scorn to be defyd/if led by Washington. (1781)

When in Love I do commence/May it be with a man of sense/Brisk and arey [airy] may he be/Free from a spirit of jealousy. (1769)

Give me a House that never will decay/ And Garments that never will wear away—/Give me a Friend that never will depart/Give me a Ruler that can rule my Heart (1792)

Beauty and Virtue when they do meet/ With a good education make a lady complete. (1724)

When this you see, remember me/And bear me in your mind./What others say when I'm away/Speak of me as you find. (1785)

When two fond hearts as one unite,/The yoke is easy and the burden light. (1822)

Please to survey this with a tender eye/Put on good nature and lay judgement by. (1815)

When I am dead and worms me eat/ Here you shall see my name complete (1787)

This I did to let you see/What care my parents took of me. (1752)

Respect to parents always must be paid/or God is angered and they are disobeyed. (1784)

The Father fled to Worlds unknown/ When aged fifty two/The Mothers left and may we all/Her virtuous steps pursue. (1805)

Now here you read that death has call my parents Dear,/and may we all for that day prepare. ((1816)

May I with innocence and peace/My tranquil moments spend/And when the toils of life shall cease/With calmness meet my end. (1810)

To Colleges and Schools ye Youths repair/Improve each precious Moment while you're there. (1786)

Delight in Learning Soon doth Bring/a Child to Learn the Hardist Thing. (1797)

Though young in age And small in stature/Yet I have skill to form a letter. (1787)

In Mother's womb Thy fingers did me make,/and from the womb Thou didst me safely take;/From breast Thou hast me nurst my life throughout./I may say I never wanted ought. (1757)

It is a pity that Lydia Kephart did not record her age on her sampler as most schoolgirls did. Though she refers to her "youthfull hands" in her verse she must have stitched many decorative needleworks before this masterpiece. Witness the mastery of her needle in her perfectly even stitches. The top border and the one that boxes the verse are remarkably symmetrical. She obviously started her vertical, fruited borders from the bottom and had to reduce the scale at the top to make the repeats come out evenly. Such "adjustments" are not at all uncommon and more frequent in American than British samplers, perhaps because American girls attempted more original designs.

Her charming design suggests that she must have loved the outdoors to judge by her lush lawnscape across the bottom done in uncouched satin stitch; the plump, satin-stitched birds; and trees and flowers everywhere.

The original, which measures 21 inches square, is from the collection of M. Finkel & Daughter.

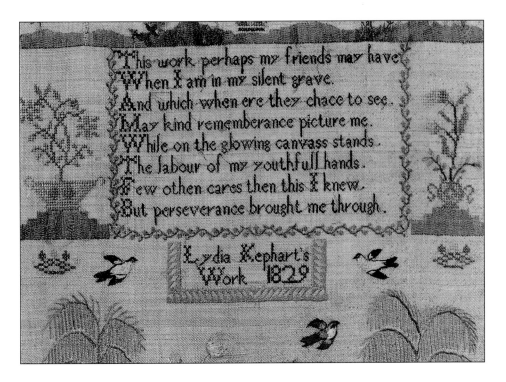

Lydia's verse appears to be original. So does her spelling ("youthfull" and "canvass") and her grammar ("chace" for "chance?" "then" for "than?").

She speaks from a stitcher's heart, certainly, hoping that the satisfaction she takes from the result of her "perseverance" may somehow be shared by others.

Her lugubrious sense of mortality, sad in one so young, is common among mottoes in schoolgirl samplers of this period.

Crochet & Knitting Abbreviations

beg	begin, beginning
CC	contrasting color
ch	chain
circ	circular
cn	cable needle
dc	double crochet
dec	decrease(s), decreasing
dp	double-point
foll	follows, following
gr	gram(s)
hdc	half double rochet
hk	hook
inc	increase(s), increasing
k	knit
k 2 tog	knit 2 together
lp	loop
MC	main color
mos	months
no	number
oz	ounce(s)
p	purl
pat	pattern
rem	remaining, remainder
rep	repeat
rnd	round
sc	single crochet
sk	skip
SKP	slip-knit-pass
sl	slip
sl	slip stich
sp	space
st(s)	stitch(es)
St st	stockinette stitch
tbl	through back loop
tog	together
tr	treble crochet
yo	yarn over
mm	millimeters
cm	centimeters

Crochet & Knitting Techniques

Chain Stitch (ch)

Make a slip knot and place on hook. * Yarn over hook and draw through loop, repeat from *.

Single Crochet (sc)

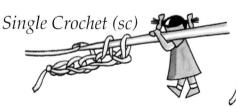

1. Insert hook into stitch, yarn over hook and draw through stitch. There are two loops on the hook.

2. Yarn over hook and draw through both loops on hook. There is one loop left.

Half Double Crochet (hdc)

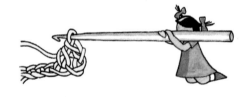

1. Yarn over hook, insert hook through stitch, yarn over hook and draw through stitch. You will have three loops on the hook.

2. Yarn over hook and draw through all three loops. You will have one loop left on the hook.

Double Crochet (dc)

1. Yarn over hook, insert hook through stitch, yarn over hook and draw through stitch. You will have three loops on the hook.

2. Yarn over hook and draw through two loops. You will have two loops on the hook.

3. Yarn over hook and draw through the remaining two loops. You will have one loop left on the hook.

Yarn Over (yo)

Wrap yarn over the right-hand needle without working into a stitch.

Knit (k)

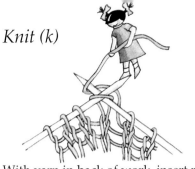

With yarn in back of work, insert right needle behind left needle up through front of stitch; wrap yarn behind and under right needle and draw through stitch; slip stitch off left needle.

Purl (p)

With yarn in front of work, insert right needle in front of left needle down through front of stitch; wrap yarn over and behind right needle and draw through stitch; slip stitch off left needle.

Increase #1 (inc)

Knit into the front loop and into the back loop of the same stitch.

Increase #2 (inc)

Knit into the stitch of the row below the next stitch on the left needle.

Binding Off

Work two stitches; * lift the former stitch over the latter stitch and off the right needle; work the next stitch and repeat from * to end. Cut yarn and draw through the last remaining loop.

Decrease #1 (dec)
Knit Two Together (k 2 tog)

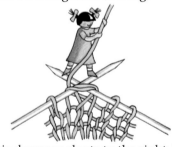

This decrease slants to the right. Insert the right needle through two stitches at the same time and knit as if they were one stitch.

Decrease #2 (dec)
Slip-Knit-Pass (SKP)

This decrease slants to the left. Slip one stitch from the left to the right needle as if to knit, knit the next stitch, pass the slipped stitch over the knitted stitch and off the right needle.

Picking up Stitches Along Bound-off or Cast-on Edges

Draw loops of yarn through stitches near edge, skipping spaces between stitches, and place on needle.

Stockinette Stitch (st st)

Row 1: Knit. Row 2: Purl. Repeat these two rows. The knit side is smooth and looks like a series of connected V's. The purl side is pebbly and tends to curl under at the edges.

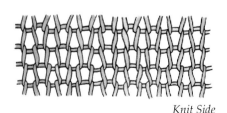

Knit Side

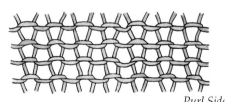

Purl Side

Picture Framing

What better way to finish a lovingly hand-crafted item than to frame it yourself? Framing an object immediately gives it a totally different look. Matting and framing are not difficult but do require precision and patience. All cutting tools must be *sharp:* the saw blade, the mat-cutter blade (keep several extras handy) and the glass cutter.

Tools and supplies are found at hardware and art-supply stores. High-quality ready-made materials are popular with time-conscious crafters. You can buy precut mats in a variety of colors in standard sizes or you can have a mat custom-cut for you to make your particular project fit a standard-sized frame. Standard sizes for mats and wood frames include 3 by 5, 5 by 7, 7 by 9, 8 by 10, 9½ by 11, 11 by 14, 12 by 16, 16 by 20 and 24 by 36 inches. Contemporary-style metal frames in gold, silver and sometimes black can be purchased in whole-inch sizes at art-supply stores. Once you assemble your tools and materials, it takes only a couple of hours to mat and frame most pieces.

Many pieces must be mounted onto some kind of backing board. If the backing board will show, use mat board or mat board covered with fabric. If it will not show, use anything handy: Foam board, clean cardboard and posterboard all work well. The backing board and mat (if you use one) should be the same size. "Free mount" refers to framing artwork using only pH-neutral materials. Acid-free or rag backing and mat boards dramatically retard decomposition of fibers. These materials cost more than non-acid-free materials, but they do help protect your artwork for generations to come.

If you are doing your own matting, before doing any serious mat cutting, take time to get the feel of your particular mat cutter. Using a ruler, draw long lines on mat board and make practice cuts, learning how to make a straight cut that stops and starts exactly where you want it to. A piece of cardboard beneath your work surface will save the tabletop and also keep your cutter blades sharp longer.

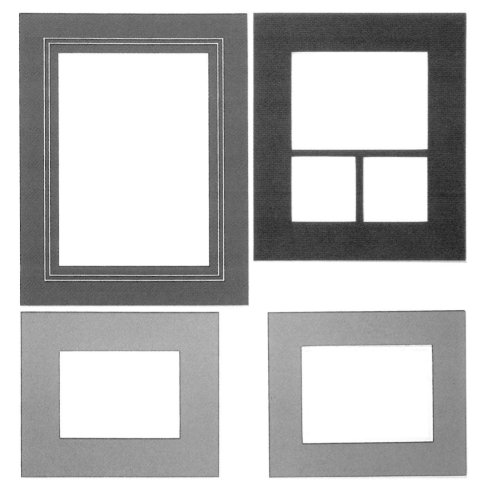

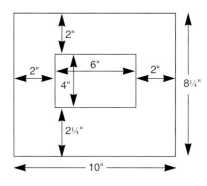

Shown clockwise from the upper left corner: Double V-groove mat, multiple opening mat, double mat, single mat.

Matting

Mat board is available in hundreds of colors and three basic types:

1. Standard three- or four-ply colored board that has a white or off-white core.

2. Acid-free or rag board, available in one-, two-, three- or four-ply.

3. Solid or colored-core mats, which are a relatively recent addition to the market—the core is colored (instead of plain white), so the beveled opening has a dramatic stripe effect.

Take your piece to the supply store with you and try it on different mat colors. The only rule is that the mat color complement the artwork.

✿ *Straight cuts allow you to make a multitude of different shapes. Circular cuts are much more difficult to master and usually require special tools.*

Ruler
Mat board
T-square
Mat cutter (not a mat or utility knife) and extra blades
Fabric (optional)
Sharp pencil; fine emery boards; double-sided clear tape; clear tape; ½" paint-brush; white glue
Single-edge razor blades

Single Mat

1. Measure your artwork and decide how big the window opening of the mat should be. Be sure the opening is at least ¼ inch smaller than the piece itself.

2. Decide how much mat you want around the window. Making the bottom a little wider than the other three sides often gives a more balanced appearance when the piece is hung on the wall, but this is a matter of preference.

3. Determine outside measurements by adding window and mat measurements as shown. Drawing a picture each time will help avoid mistakes. Double check! This is the trickiest part.

4. Draw a box with outside measurements on wrong side of mat board, using a T-square for accuracy. Check to be sure corners are true. With cutter blade vertical, use T-square as a guide and cut out box.

5. On wrong side of mat, draw window box. Extend lines at each corner slightly to show intersection clearly. Angle blade in mat cutter to cut bevel. Using T-square as a guide, cut one line of the window box, extending cut 1/16 inch beyond each corner.

6. Remove cutter and T-square, turn mat counterclockwise and cut next side. Repeat this procedure until all four sides are cut. Don't cut sides out of turn. Window piece should fall out when mat is picked up. If it doesn't, cut corners by hand with single-edge razor blade. Don't pull corners out—they will tear.

7. If the cut or the corners aren't perfect, touch up with a fine emery board.

Double Mat

1. Select two colors. Decide which will be the top and which will be the bottom mat. Decide how much of the bottom mat you want to show (¼ inch is standard, but by no means universal). Follow steps 1 to 3 for Single Mat.

2. Draw a picture showing all dimensions. Add mat and window dimensions to determine outside measurements. Using T-square and vertical cutter blade, cut two boxes with outside measurements, one from each color.

3. Cut the top color mat as in step 5 for Single Mat. Place double-sided clear tape around back side of top mat, close to outside edges. Place bottom mat with right side facing tape. Make outside edges of both mats line up together.

4. Place window piece from top mat back in center until bottom mat is cut (this gives a better cutting surface). Cut bottom mat as in step 5 for Single Mat, being sure bottom edges of both mats correspond. Remove window pieces.

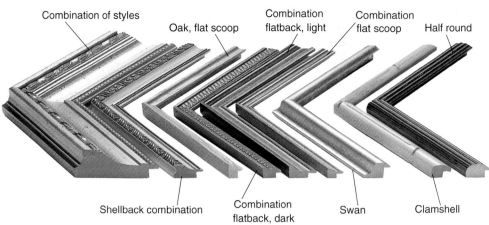

Combination of styles
Oak, flat scoop
Combination flatback, light
Combination flat scoop
Half round
Shellback combination
Combination flatback, dark
Swan
Clamshell

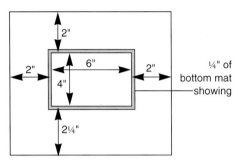

2"
2"
6"
2"
4"
¼" of bottom mat showing
2¼"

Multiple-Opening Mat
Once you've mastered the Single Mat, a Multiple-Opening Mat is easy. As a general rule, the mat border between the individual windows should be narrower than the mat border surrounding all the windows.

1. Draw a picture of what the mat should look like. Include all dimensions. Determine outside measurements by adding all horizontal dimensions and all vertical dimensions. Double check all measurements.

2. Follow steps 4 to 7 for Single Mat for each opening of the mat. Draw all openings on the back of the mat before cutting, but cut only one opening at a time. If you try to cut more than one opening at once, you may lose your place and make some bevels go the wrong way.

V-Groove Mat
This mat looks as though a shallow cut was made all the way around the window. Actually, two bevels are cut and placed facing each other to give a router-type effect. Directions are for a single V-groove; if you want more than one, draw them in and cut them out.

1. Make a drawing of the mat showing all dimensions and placement of the V-groove. (A standard placement is a third of the mat width).

2. Cut a box with outside dimensions, following step 4 for Single Mat. On the back, draw a box for the V-groove and a box for the window opening.

3. Cut V-groove box following steps 5 and 6 for Single Mat. When window mat piece falls out, turn it over so right side is up. Using T-square as a guide, carefully bevel the very edge of each side of the V-groove window piece. Fit it back into the mat, taping it in place on the back with clear tape.

4. Following steps 5 to 7 for Single Mat, cut box for image window.

Framing
Frames, or moldings, are available in thousands of styles. Wood moldings can be purchased in a variety of finishes, including all types of stain, gold leaf, silver leaf, paint, plastic laminate and wood inlay. Metal frames come in many colors and three finishes: shiny, matte and brushed. Wood moldings come from the mill in lengths ranging from 6 to 10 feet. Metal moldings come in similar lengths, but unless you have a good metal saw, you should buy your frames precut to size.

When deciding what type of frame to select, consider the artwork you are framing: style, size and colors. Contemporary artwork is often enhanced by a metal frame; needlepoint usually is not. Don't try to make a ½-inch-wide molding hold a 3- by 4-foot print and its required glass—it won't. Look for what pleases your eye and makes common sense as well, and you can't go wrong.

Determining How Much Molding to Buy
Measure the size of your frame between rabbets. An 8- by 10-inch frame made from 1¼-inch molding will be used as an example. To the width and length add ⅛ inch for clearance (frame must actually be 8⅛ by 10⅛ inches). To estimate how much molding to buy, first add the linear measurements of all four sides together (8⅛ + 8⅛ + 10⅛ + 10⅛ = 36½ inches). Add 8 times the width of the molding to allow for the miter cuts (8 x ¼ = 2 inches), then add 1 inch to allow for the kerfs, or saw cuts. So, an 8- by 10-inch frame requires 39½ inches of molding. Molding is sold by the running foot, so 4 feet would be purchased. Inspect molding carefully for imperfections before buying.

Molding
Finishing nails
Miter box and saw
2 C-clamps
Miter clamp (at least 1 but preferably 4)
Drill and bits (bit should be 25% smaller than diameter of nail)
Tack hammer
Nail set
Wax scratch-repair stick, same color as molding
Sharp pencil; ruler accurate to ¹⁄₁₆" increments; no. 80 sandpaper; wood glue

Cutting the Miter
1. Fasten miter box securely to work table with C-clamps or screws.

2. With pencil, mark for a miter at extreme right (with rabbet edge toward you) of molding. Measure along rabbet for one cut. At end of each cut make an opposite miter mark to begin next cut. Mark cutting lines for all pieces on rabbet.

3. With back of molding against fence of miter box, gently saw the miter using very light pressure and many repetitions (sawing quickly with greater pressure may result in a miter that just won't join well).

4. Reset the guide and make the opposite miter for that piece. Always use the outside of the kerf to measure from.

5. Cut all pieces. Place like-sized pieces back to back to insure uniformity. If necessary, sand one end of a too-long piece to make a matching pair.

Assembly

1. Number pieces on back in order of joining (long, short, long, short). Before joining, check each corner by clamping with miter clamp and inspecting the joint. If any touch-up sanding must be done, do it now, before joining.

If you have four miter clamps, glue all four corners and then nail all four corners. If you have only one miter clamp, glue and then nail each corner before going to the next.

2. Insert pieces 1 and 2 into miter clamp. Put wood glue on one miter of the joint, then tighten down clamp just enough to hold the corner in place securely. Immediately wipe off any excess glue: Don't let it dry on the surface of the molding. Join all four corners in order.

3. Usually, two nails per corner are sufficient. Drill a hole for each nail to avoid splitting the molding. Nails should be long enough to go through one miter and well into the next. Holes should be 25% smaller than the diameter of the nail and should go through one miter and slightly into the next. Put one nail on each side of each miter, being sure to place nails so they don't cross within the joint. Tap nails into holes and recess slightly with nail set.

4. Touch up miter joints and nail holes with wax scratch-repair sticks.

If your frame is small or the piece is lightweight, you don't have to use nails at all. They are an extra security measure only—the glue actually holds the joint.

Glass

Glass and Plexiglas are manufactured in many qualities and types. Picture-quality glass is thinner ($1/16$- versus $1/8$-inch thick) and has fewer bubbles than window glass. For framing, try to get picture-quality clear or nonglare glass or Plexiglas. Nonglare products distort images and alter colors very slightly but do allow images to be easily seen in all lightings (especially very bright rooms, where the image is usually difficult to view from almost any angle). Don't use nonglare products in shadow box or needlework applications.

Plexiglas is very lightweight, so for safety reasons it is often the best choice for very large pieces. It is also popular for clip-type frames (frames with no real sides, just glass, backing board and clips to hold it all together) because no sharp glass edges are exposed. Plexiglas does scratch easily, however, and must be cleaned with plastic cleaner, not glass cleaner, and special cloths.

Ultraviolet filtering glass is available for pieces that are susceptible to damage from exposure to light but is extremely expensive and must be purchased from art-supply stores or commercial framing establishments.

Glass
Glass cutter
Ruler; felt-tip pen; heavy work gloves

1. Mark dimensions onto glass with felt-tip pen. In one stroke, lightly score glass surface with glass cutter (pushing heavily on cutter makes glass harder to cut and tends to fracture edges) using T-square as a guide.

2. Wearing work gloves, quickly snap off glass excess. Do this immediately after scoring: Glass heals itself after being scored, and 1 minute can make the difference between a perfectly clean cut and a choppy mess.

Fitting

Artwork
Mat and backing board
Glass cut to size
Glass cleaner
Frame
$5/8$" brads
Scrap-wood block
Backing paper larger than frame
2 screw eyes
Braided wire: length $1\frac{1}{2}$ times width of frame
2 felt bumpers
Nail set; tack hammer; white glue; ruler; single-edge razor blade

1. Mount artwork within mat (if mat is used) with clear tape. If artwork is needlework, see page 23 for specific information. If no mat is used, mount artwork to chosen backing board. Make a sandwich of mat, artwork and backing board. Set aside.

2. Clean one side of glass, turn over and clean other side twice (this side will be inside the frame). Brush off any lint. Lay artwork sandwich face down on top of clean glass.

3. Brush off inside edges of frame and lay frame face down on worktable. Carefully place glass-artwork sandwich face down into frame. Pick up frame and check glass front to be sure no dirt has gotten between glass and artwork.

4. Insert one brad midway across each side. Begin brads by pressing into molding with back of nail set. Clamp a scrap wood block to edge of workbench. Brace frame against this block and tap brads in with tack hammer. Place a brad on either side of each corner and about 4 inches apart along the sides.

5. Cut a piece of backing paper larger than frame. (Backing paper can be kraft paper, old grocery bags or gift-wrapping paper. Its purpose is to keep dust out of the back of the frame.) Put a thin layer of white glue along back edge of frame. Lay paper on top and smooth down. Allow to dry and trim excess with single-edge razor blade.

6. Insert screw eyes on back edge of frame a third of the way down from the top. Thread braided wire through screw eyes and twist together tightly. Glue a felt bumper to each bottom corner to protect walls.

Wool is not harmed by high temperatures or water alone; rather, it is the combination of heat, water and the agitation of wool in water that causes felting, or shrinkage and condensation, of the fibers. 🐑 Wool is easy to spin because its natural grease, lanolin, allows the fibers to pull and glide past each other. 🐑 Wool is classified by its "count." A fine Crossbred or Romney with a 48 to 50 count is easy to spin. Fine Merino wool has a count up to 90 and is definitely for the expert. 🐑 Each breed of sheep produces its own characteristic wool, varying from short to long and fine to coarse and hairy. Generally speaking, spin soft wool for garments and coarser wool for floor rugs, etc. 🐑 In woolen yarn, all fibers are thoroughly mixed and lie in all directions, creating a soft, fluffy yarn ideal for sweaters. In worsted yarn, the fibers are basically parallel, making a stronger, firmer yarn to use for items like socks or mittens that get more direct wear. 🐑 The natural presence of lanolin in wool makes spinning great for the hands. If a sheep is nicked while being sheared, lanolin helps heal the sheep's skin. 🐑 An experienced shearer can shear 100 sheep in a day—and he'll be covered with lanolin from head to toe when he's done. 🐑 Black sheep are often kept in the barn on clear days so their wool won't become sun-bleached. 🐑 Handwashed homespuns always retain a certain amount of natural lanolin that "turns" both wind and rain, making the garments very desirable for outdoor wear. 🐑 Talcum powder on your hands and needles makes slippery wool easier to knit. 🐑 When "waste not, want not" was a way of life, every part of the fleece would be used. When fleece was washed, lanolin floated to the top of the wash water and was skimmed off; lanolin was used as a moisturizing and protective lotion for the skin. The wash and rinse waters, which contained quite a bit of manure from the fleece, were used for the garden. The noils, small bits and pieces that could not be spun, were used to stuff pillows. 🐑 "Spinning in the grease" means to spin from a fleece that has had no preparation; few fleeces lend themselves to this. 🐑 If wool is slightly warmed or placed in the sun, it spins more easily. 🐑 If wool is dyed before it is spun, lanolin must be added so the wool will spin well.

Two-ply black and light wool carded together

Two-ply nubbly light

Two-ply dark

One-ply light

Clothing, Accessories & Home Decor

Leafing through the projects in this section is like opening an old trunk in a sunlit attic. Out of it cascade:

- Charming bibs for babies,
- Elegant evening bags,
- Native American beadwork,
- Three darling dollhouse rugs, (using three different skills),
- Tatted Victorian boxes,
- Classic Italian *trapunto* work and more.

It is a tour back through time to revisit precious traditional designs and techniques. Some, almost lost forever, have been preserved in how-to diagrams and step-by-step instructions you will find among the 42 charming project designs in this section for home and wardrobe (including some *very* appealing teddy bears).

Seascape Bib

B ibs suffer little abrasive wear and are forgiving in their fit. They can be used frequently and passed down through the family for another child to wear. For many adults, the pattern and designs on a bib form one of their earliest visual memories of childhood. If you are making one for your own child, you may want to match the colors with a best dress-up outfit.

Create this restful scene of sea and sky, sailboat and gulls in blue and yellow matte fabric with appliqué and glossy embroidered details. The scalloped edges are carefully finished with blanket stitch to frame the picture. Embroider the bib with satin stitch, stem stitch and blanket stitch (see pages 14 and 15). The finished bib measures 8 by 10½ inches.

11 by 14" piece lightweight closely woven linen or cotton fabric, white or other background color
Fabric scraps for appliqué, yellow and light blue
Fusible appliqué backing
6-strand embroidery floss, 1 skein each of yellow and light blue
Cotton sewing thread to match fabric
⅜" cotton twill tape, 24" long
Pencil for marking fabric
Embroidery hoop
Iron, to transfer design on bound-in sheet

Marking Fabric

In the center of the white fabric, lightly mark an 8- by 10½-inch rectangle. Very lightly, transfer the pattern printed on the large bound-in pattern sheet provided. Place the scalloped bottom and sides along the bottom and sides of the marked rectangle. After ironing on the the edges and motifs, complete the scallops at the top by hand. Lightly transfer markings for the large gull and boat sail to yellow fabric; boat to blue fabric. The bib itself is not to be cut until the appliqué and all embroidery, except the edging, are completed.

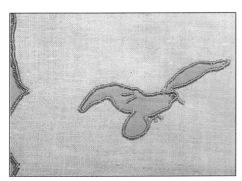

Here is a close-up view of the large gull and the scalloped edge. The satin-stitch outlines and details are worked in a satin stitch so tiny and close that the stitches form a little ridge on the fabric surface.

Very small blanket stitches made with sewing thread join the boat and the side edges of its sail to the bib. The top and bottom edges of the sail and mast are in a satin stitch. Appliqué requires patience and care, but the results are worth the effort.

Birds and Waves

Use two strands of embroidery floss for all embroidery stitches.

1. Carefully cut out the shape of the large bird from the yellow fabric and fusible appliqué backing. Do not turn edges under. Simply use fusible appliqué backing and press into place.

Place in an embroidery hoop. With close satin stitches, embroider the blue outlines and yellow beak and claws.

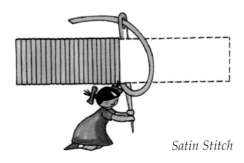

Satin Stitch

2. Embroider the smaller background birds with blue satin-stitch wings and yellow satin-stitch bodies.

3. Embroider the waves in stem stitch with blue embroidery floss.

Boat

1. Carefully cut out the shapes for the boat (blue fabric) and its sail (yellow fabric), adding ⅛ inch around all edges. Cut boat and sail shapes from fusible appliqué backing. Turn fabric edges under ⅛ inch and fuse pieces in place onto background fabric.

※ *The small blue boat piece may be embroidered with long satin stitches rather than being appliquéd.*

2. Using the sewing thread, work a blanket stitch along the side edges of the sail and all around the boat.

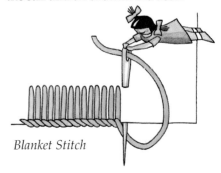

Blanket Stitch

3. Finish the top and bottom edges of the sail with small, close yellow satin stitches. Embroider the mast using a small satin stitch.

Edging and Finishing

1. Cut out the bib. With the bib folded in half lengthwise, cut an opening for the neck that is 2 inches deep at the center and 1¾ inches wide while still folded. (The finished opening will be 3½ inches wide and 2 inches deep.)

Without the embroidery hoop, work around the entire scalloped edge closely in a blanket stitch, using blue floss.

2. Cut the twill tape in half to make two 12-inch ties. Sew ends securely to opposite sides of the neck opening.

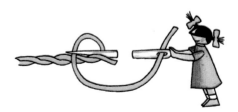

Stem Stitch

Child's Pullover

9 (10, 11, 12)"

3½ (4, 4½, 5)"

6 (6½, 7, 7½)"

11 (12, 13, 14)"

There is no doubt about it—red is cheerful. It brightens even the palest complexion. If you don't know the sex of an unborn sweater recipient, red is one of the more interesting "compromise" colors. It also may make it easier, one day, for you to pick out your child in a huddle of baby blues and pinks, at nursery school or the day care center. This sweater is easier to make than it looks because the rocking horse design is cross-stitched into a plain knitted panel afterward rather than knitted into the panel directly.

Because these motifs are cross-stitched onto the sweater rather than knit into the garment, you could buy a sweater, then add the rocking horses.

See page 44 for knitting abbreviations.

Knitting instructions are given for 6 months size, with changes for 12 months, 18 months and 24 months sizes in parentheses. Finished chest measurements are 22 (24, 26, 28) inches.

Sport-weight yarn: two 1¾-oz (50-gr) skeins MC (we used red), 1 skein CC (we used white)
6-strand embroidery floss: 1 skein each blue and red or desired colors
Knitting needles size 4 and 2 or one pair to knit the indicated gauge and one pair two sizes smaller
1 stitch holder
1 tapestry needle

Determining Correct Gauge

6 sts = 1", 8 rows = 1", working in St st. To ensure correct finished measurements, take time to check gauge. Make a sample swatch: With the larger size needles, cast on 24 sts. Work in St st for 32 rows. Lay swatch flat and measure it. Without bunching or stretching, swatch should be 4" square. If swatch is too big, try again with smaller needles; if too small, try larger needles.

The Back

With smaller needles and MC, cast on 60 (66, 72, 78) sts. Work in k 1, p 1 ribbing for 1½", inc 6 sts evenly spaced across last rib row—66 (72, 78, 84) sts. Change to larger needles and St st. Work even until back measures 6 (6½,

7, 7½)" from beg or desired length to underarm, end on wrong side ready for a k row.

Shape Back Armholes

Bind off 5 sts at beg of next 2 rows—56 (62, 68, 74) sts. Dec 1 st at each end of next row—54 (60, 66, 72) sts. Work even until armhole measures 3½ (4, 4½, 5)", end on wrong side ready for a k row.

Shape Back Shoulders

Bind off 7 (8, 9, 10) sts at beg of next 4 rows—26 (28, 30, 32) sts. Sl rem sts to holder for back of neck.

The Front

Work in the same manner as the back until armhole measures ¼" deep, cut MC. Join CC and work even for 16 (18, 22, 24) rows, cut CC. Join MC and work even until armhole measures 2¾ (3, 3½, 3¾)", end on wrong side, ready for a k row.

Shape Front Neck

Divide Work: K 14 (16, 18, 20), bind off next 26 (28, 30, 32) sts for center front neck edge, k rem sts—14 (16, 18, 20) sts each side.

Next Row: P 14 (16, 18, 20), drop yarn, join another ball of MC and p rem 14 (16, 18, 20) sts.

Work even across both groups of sts each row until front armhole measures same as back, end on wrong side, ready for a k row.

Shape Front Shoulders

Working across both groups of sts each row, bind off 7 (8, 9, 10) sts at beg of next 4 rows. Fasten.

The Sleeve

Instructions are given for both a puffed sleeve cap (girl's sweater) and a plain set-in sleeve cap (boy's or girl's sweater).

With smaller size needles and MC, cast on 45 (47, 50, 52) sts. Work in k 1, p 1 ribbing for 1", inc 12 sts evenly spaced across last rib row—57 (59, 62, 64) sts. Work even until sleeve measures 2 (2¼, 2½, 2¾)" from beg, end on wrong side ready for a k row.

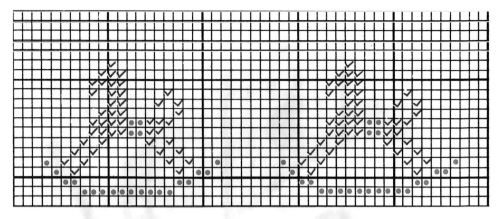

Each square of the graph represents a knitted stitch. Work cross-stitch in horizontal rows, left to right or right to left. Each "X" of the cross-stitch covers a "V" of the knitted fabric. All sizes have two embroidered rocking horses, 5 sts apart, centered top to bottom and side to side in the white panel. Note that for all sizes there is one stitch more to the right of the design than to the left. Count carefully to place the design correctly.

Finishing the Garment

With tapestry needle and yarn, sew side, shoulder and sleeve seams. Set in sleeves, gathering fullness of puffed sleeve cap at shoulder or easing in fullness of plain set-in cap.

Back and Side Neck Edging
With right side of work facing, using MC and smaller size needles, pick up 15 (16, 17, 18) sts along right front neck edge, k the 26 (28, 30, 32) sts of back neck edge from holder, pick up 15 (16, 17, 18) sts along left front neck edge—56 (60, 64, 68) sts. Working in k 1, p 1 ribbing, k tog the first and last 2 sts of every other row twice—52 (56, 60, 64) sts. Bind off loosely in ribbing.

Front Neck Edging
With right side of work facing, using MC and smaller size needles, pick up 1 st in each of 26 (28, 30, 32) bound-off sts of front neck edge. Working in k 1, p 1 ribbing, k tog the first and last 2 sts of every other row twice—22 (24, 26, 28) sts. Bind off in ribbing at even tension. Sew neck edging seams.

Puffed Sleeve Cap Only
Bind off 5 sts at beg of next 2 rows—47 (49, 52, 54) sts. Dec 1 st each end of next row—45 (47, 50, 52) sts. Work even until cap measures 2 (2½, 3, 3½)".
Dec Row: K 2 tog, k 1, k 2 tog, k to last 5 sts, end k 2 tog, k 1, k 2 tog—2 sts taken off each end.
Next Row: P across. Rep these 2 rows 7 times more—13 (15, 18, 20) sts.

Last Row: K 2 tog across and bind off at the same time. Fasten.
Plain Set-in Sleeve Cap Only
Bind off 5 sts at beg of next 2 rows—47 (49, 52, 54) sts.
Single Decrease Row: K 1, SKP, k to last 3 sts, end k 2 tog, k 1—1 st taken off each end.
Next Row: P across.
Rep these 2 rows 2 (2, 5, 8) times more—41 (43, 40, 36) sts.
Double Decrease Row: K 1, s1 2, k 1, pass both s1 sts over, k to last 4 sts, end k 3 tog, k 1—2 sts taken off each end.
Next Row: P across.
Rep these 2 rows 7 (7, 6, 5) times more—9 (11, 12, 12) sts. Bind off rem sts, fasten.

Embroidering the Horses

Following embroidery chart, above, with tapestry needle and six strands of embroidery floss, work the design in cross-stitch. Each "X" of the cross-stitch covers one "V" of the knitted fabric. Keep embroidery tension fairly slack to avoid bunching the fabric. (See page 15 for directions for cross-stitch.)

Close-up of the rocking horse panel. The white background is a knitted-in stockinette stitch stripe on the sweater front. Embroider the horses on before sewing the garment together, using six strands of shiny cotton embroidery floss and the cross-stitch.

This close-up reveals that a properly executed cross-stitch on the right side of the fabric shows up as a lone vertical on the wrong side. If you catch the loose ends of your working strand under a few embroidered stitches as you go, you will save having to weave them in later.

Evening Collar & Bag

A touch of lace gives a dress or sweater a romantic Victorian look. This versatile crocheted-lace collar can be worn with the pearl-buttoned opening at the back, front or shoulder. The collar can be blocked to fit either a round, oval or V-shaped neckline. Add the flirtatious little purse for feminine appeal.

Linen-Lace Collar and Bag

See the photo of the linen-lace collar and bag shown opposite. See page 44 for crochet abbreviations.

20/1 natural unbleached linen thread
No. 5 metal crochet hook
Fastener for collar: 2 pearl buttons, ⅜"
For bag: ribbon, twill tape or cord (for drawstring)

To Make the Collar

Ch 185, turn, dc into 3rd ch st.

Row 1: Dc into each ch st, ch 3, turn.

Row 2: Repeat row 1.

Row 3: Dc into each ch st, ch 2, turn.

Row 4: Sc into 2nd dc and each dc increasing by 1 st in every 10th dc. Ch 2, turn.

Row 5: Repeat row 4 but omit ch 2 at end, turn.

Row 6: Ch 5, sc into 3rd sc, rep to end of row. Ch 3, turn.

Row 7: Sc into 3rd sc, * ch 5, sc into 3rd sc, rep from * to end, ch 3, sc into end sc, ch 2, turn.

Row 8: Sc into 2nd sc, sc into each ch st skipping each sc at lace joins (i. e., sc in 4, skip 1, sc in 4, skip 1, rep to end), ch 3, turn.

Row 9: Dc into 2nd sc, dc into each sc.

Finishing the Collar

Ch 5 for buttonhole loop, sl st into top of row 9 dc. Sl st several times up the collar edge to bottom of row 1 dc, ch 5 (for buttonhole loop) sl st into top of row 1 dc. Tie off tightly with beginning thread. Clip tied ends close. Sew two antique or new pearl buttons onto other edge of collar to match loops and overlap collar edges as you need.

If you would like to sew the collar directly onto the clothing neckline, preshrink collar and clothing fabrics before attaching. Use a sewing thread that does not quite match to attach collar so that if you want to remove it later you will not accidently cut the delicate crochet thread.

To Make the Bag

Ch 63.

Row 1: Sc into each ch st, ch 2, turn.

Rows 2 and 3: Repeat row 1.

Row 4: * Ch 9, sc into 3rd sc, repeat from *. Ch 4, turn.

Row 5: * Sc into middle (st 5) of chained loop, ch 3, repeat from *.

Row 6: Sc into each st (each ch and each sc), ch 2, turn.

Row 7: Sc into each sc, ch 2, turn.

Row 8: * Ch 5, sc into every 2nd sc, repeat *, ch 4 to end, turn.

Rows 9–11: Dc in every st, ch 4, turn.

Row 12: Dc in every st, ch 2, turn.

Rows 13–16: Sc in every st, ch 2, turn.

Row 17: Repeat row 4.

Row 18: Repeat row 5.

Rows 19–22: Sc in each st.

Finishing the Bag

Fold piece in half to form a tube, with row 1 at top and row 22 at bottom. Sl st across bottom to turned side and then back across bottom (for strength) to the open side. Continue sl st up the open side and tie off at top. Insert ribbon, twill tape or cord through lace area of rows 4 and 5 for strap.

Cotton-Lace Collar

Notice how this delicate cotton collar can lend a lacy elegance to anything—even this page!

Knit-Cro-Sheen in desired color and weight
No. 7 crochet hook
Fastener: hook and eye, small button or Velcro

Chain 128, turn.

Row 1: Dc in each ch st, ch 3, turn.

Row 2: Skip first dc. *Dc 3 in 2nd dc, ch 5. Rep from * to end, finish with dc in beg ch 3. Ch 3, turn.

Row 3: * Dc 2, ch 1, dc 2 in 2nd dc of group of 3, ch 5. Rep from * to end, finish with dc in beg ch. Ch 3, turn.

Row 4: * Dc 5 in ch 1, ch 2, sc over ch 5 in row 2 and row 3 together, ch 2, rep from * around. Finish each row in same way. Ch 3, turn.

Row 5: * Dc 3, ch 1, dc 3 in 3rd dc of group, ch 5, rep from * to end, ch 3, turn.

Row 6: * Dc 7 in ch 1 space, ch 5, rep from * to end, ch 3, turn.

Row 7: * Dc 8 in 4th dc of group, ch 2, sc over ch 5 of rows 5 and 6 together, ch 2, rep from * to end. Fasten off.

Fasten the collar with a hook and eye, a button and loop or Velcro.

The dressy cotton-lace collar shown full size on this page was made with lightweight Knit-Cro-Sheen. If you want a more substantial look to go with a bulky sweater or casual dress, use a heavier weight thread, as shown in the detail at left.

Victorian Purses

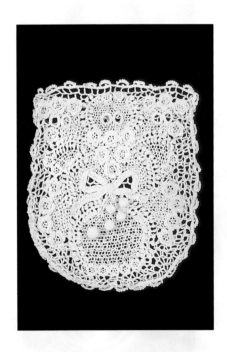

"No lady of fashion appears in public without her *reticule* which should contain her handkerchief and fan, card-money and essence-bottle." So reads a fashion article of 1808. Reticules are little bags made of silk, velvet, netting or tapestry, often embellished with intricate embroidery or beading. Enjoy the inspiring 19th- and early 20th-century examples shown here and on the following pages, and create a replica of the circa 1870 reticule shown on page 61.

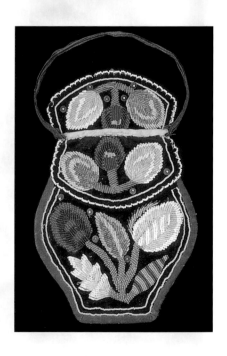

Reticule means "a network," probably because early ones were often crocheted of silk thread or constructed of other net material, like the 1847 net and silk handkerchief bag, given to Martha A. Chapin Wilcox by her Uncle Shepherd on the day of her marriage (*below, left*). Reticules were handmade for special occasions, like the patriotic satin drawstring bag (*below, center*).

These jaunty little drawstring bags were so popular during the late 18th and early 19th centuries that they were sometimes called "indispensables." They came into their own during the Empire period when the lightweight, flowing fashions would not support underpockets, causing, by necessity, a revival of the bags carried by Greek women in classical times. Often reticules were shaped to resemble Etruscan vases (*like the urn-shaped bags at the left and on page 60*). Beaded bags were so much in vogue during the 1920s that kits were available for making them at home. Women had several reticules to match or coordinate with dresses and carried them by their drawing cords or fastened them to their waistbands with a brooch. A more informal contemporary lady of fashion might attach her reticule to a belt loop on her Levi's or Calvin Klein's.

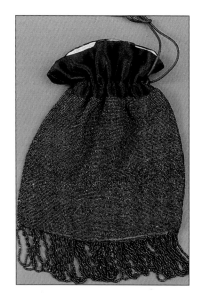

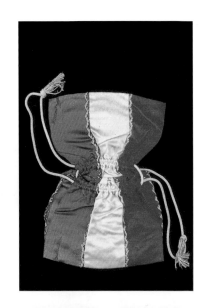

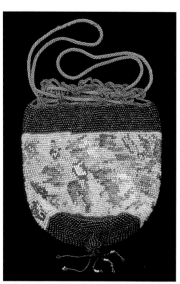

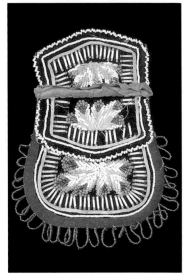

3. To make closure strap, fold one 8-inch length of ribbon under ¼ inch on each narrow end and stitch. Fold ends under ½ inch and stitch again. Sew snaps securely to ribbon ends. Topstitch center of strip to center back of reticule 2 inches from top edge, making a small neat rectangle of stitches.

4. Baste right sides of reticule fabric together with tassel sandwiched inside so that the tassel top is caught at the junction of all seams. Stitch, starting and ending at reticule top, being careful not to catch closure straps in seams. Trim seams and turn right side out. Sew lining in same manner as reticule. Leave inside out.

5. Make handle strap by folding ends of 9-inch ribbon under ¼ inch and stitch. Thread ribbon ends through one metal ring on each end and stitch again to secure ring. Slip 3-inch ribbons through handle rings so that ribbon ends are even; stitch ends together.

6. Fold top of reticule and lining under ¼ inch to wrong sides and press. Place lining inside reticule, being careful to match seams (wrong sides together). Sandwich one handle strap end between layers at center front and top-stitch. When you reach center back, insert other handle end; finish topstitching.

7. Slip-stitch decorative braid to all four side seams. Slip-stitch braid around top, overlapping at center side. Fold side pieces of bag in, as shown, encircle bag with closure ribbon and snap to close.

¼ yard velvet, brocade, satin or other fabric for reticule (2 coordinating fabrics may be used, as in the one shown here)
¼ yard contrasting satin or other material for lining
¾ yard good-quality grosgrain ribbon, ½" wide, for fastener and handle
1 silk drapery tassel
2 steel or brass rings for handle, ½" diameter
1½ yards narrow braiding for trim
Thread to match fabric; ¼" snap for closure

 Allow extra material for fabric matching if necessary.

1. Using full-size pattern provided, cut four pieces from reticule fabric (or two from each coordinating fabric). Cut four pieces from lining fabric. Cut one 8-inch, one 9-inch and two 3-inch pieces of ribbon.

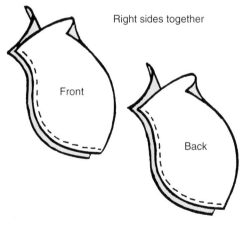

Right sides together

Front

Back

2. With right sides of reticule fabric together, stitch front to one side piece on one side only. Stitch back to other side piece as shown. Trim all seams, clip curves and press open.

The four-sided circa 1870 reticule shown here is easily adapted for contemporary use. It can be as dressed up or down as you like. Almost any firm-bodied fabric will do, including tapestry or petit point. Drapery or upholstery samples are ideal. The original has two coordinating fabrics, a black-and-gold brocade and a striped satin. The decorative linked-metal beading is hand sewn onto the seams. You may want to use a pretty narrow braid instead. The handle and closure straps are sewn from thin satin strips. Our instructions call for grosgrain ribbon, or you can make your own strips from fabric remnants. You may want to add jet (black) or other beads, or decorative needlework for interest. See the reticules on pages 58 and 59 for inspiration. Do any needle- or beadwork before final construction.

Is this the cat that ate the canary? Our needlepoint Tabby won't tell, but he will tell us that he's a direct descendant of a popular early-20th-century fabric doorstop that has regained popularity in the past few years. A penchant for fine-feathered entrées seems to run in

Doorstop Cat

the family, as you'll see in the photo of Tabby's great grandfather shown opposite. If you're browsing in antiques shops, look for Tabby's other ancestors, or produce your own tabby in needlepoint, using instructions that follow and the full-size chart on the pattern sheet.

This original early-20th-century fabric cat has his front, back and underside printed on the fabric so that however and wherever he's seated, his details will show.

13-mesh canvas, 13 by 15"
3-ply Persian wool in the following colors
(numbers given are for Paternayan wool;
number of strands given for 33-inch-
long strands):
   White—261; 2 strands
   Charcoal—222; 54 strands
   Golden brown—445; 32 strands
   Khaki brown—454; 50 strands
   Wicker brown—498; 1 strand (for eye)
½ yard fabric, in desired color, for backing
Thread to match
Polyester fiberfill
4 cups sand
Plastic bag
Cardboard

See page 16 for stitch instructions; see the Hints on page 65, for helpful tips.

1. Following full-size chart on pattern page, and using two strands of yarn throughout, stitch cat design in basketweave as much as possible; fill in remaining small areas with basic half cross-stitch.

2. Block your finished needlepoint work by stretching and pinning it into shape onto an ironing board. Gently steam, holding iron above, not on, the work. Allow work to dry completely before unpinning.

3. From backing fabric, cut a 13- by 15-inch piece. Place fabric face down on the right side of the needlepoint. Pin the fabric to the needlepoint canvas.

✱ *If you use a napped fabric for your backing, make certain that the nap is smooth from top to bottom.*

4. Working with the wrong side of the needlepoint facing up, machine-stitch through both layers, starting at the bottom corner of the design and working up and around the head and down to the remaining corner. Reinforce details of the head area by running a second row of stitching over the first, beginning at the neck and ending on the opposite side of the neck. The sewing machine needle should just pierce the edge stitches of the needlepoint.

5. Turn canvas right side out and carefully push out the ears and curves. Begin stuffing the ears. Pack ears very firmly with fiberfill and continue filling down to the paws (the entire cat should be firmly packed). Set aside.

6. Fill plastic bag with sand and squeeze out all the air so that the bag will conform to the shape of the design. Tie the bag carefully. The sand bag should just fill the remaining space in the bottom of cat. Adjust the amount of fiberfill to accommodate the sand bag. Set sand bag aside for the moment.

7. Using full-size pattern provided, cut a cardboard base. From remaining fabric, cut a piece at least 1½ inches larger than the pattern. Placing the cardboard on the wrong side of the fabric, run a gathering thread around the edge of the fabric and pull up tightly so that the cardboard is covered smoothly and neatly. Knot thread.

8. At lower edge of cat, turn unworked canvas back to wrong side of work and loosely stitch into place by hand. Fold up remaining edge of backing fabric along base. Check evenness by standing the cat up, making certain it does not lean. Place the sand bag into bottom of cat and check for firmness, evenness (balance) and uniformity of filling.

9. Place fabric-covered cardboard base in position and pin securely. With matching double-ply thread, blind-stitch base to body of cat.

Use this color photo of the painted canvas as a color guide.

Navajo Designs

Interior decorators and designers have rediscovered the beauty of the colors and motifs of the American Southwest. Popular color schemes reflect the desert landscape, from the rust, tan and gray of sand and rock to the clear turquoise blue of the Southwestern sky. The Navajo motifs shown on these pages depict god's-eyes and other Navajo symbols from northern Arizona.

The ancient god's-eye symbol traveled from Central America through Mexico to the Southwestern United States centuries ago. Originally, medicine men wove a god's-eye of yarn or string on two sticks for each newborn baby. Navajos believed this talisman would ward off blindness caused by an eye disease then rampant among their people. The disease is now controlled by antibiotics, but the god's-eye motif is still used to decorate Navajo homes.

Select a single design from the Navajo Sampler shown opposite to make needle-point pillows or wall hangings. To create a 15-inch square pillow, enlarge the color "sampler" design on the facing page by 300% on a photocopier. The marriage of needlepoint with ancient symbols is an especially happy one.

The Persian yarn colors used in the 14-inch square pillow shown in the photo above are: 40 yards rust; 25 yards gray; 30 yards ecru; 12 yards black; 55 yards tan. Also, 15-inch-square rust velveteen fabric; 3 yards each rust, tan, black yarn for tassels (optional); 5 feet twisted cord (optional).

For the Sampler Pillow:

Persian yarn: 15 yards turquoise; 14 yards ochre; 10 yards dark brown; 33 yards rust; 120 yards desired color for background
20" square white mono needlepoint canvas, 12 mesh per inch
15" square velveteen fabric for back
Masking tape
Waterproof marking pen (optional)
No. 18 tapestry needle
Sewing thread to match
Polyester fiberfill
Scissors (sharp, narrow point); ruler; artist's stretcher strips to make frame (optional); staple gun (optional); clear nail polish; pins; steam iron

1. Bind raw edges of canvas with masking tape to prevent raveling. Measure 4¾ inches down from center of canvas for first stitch; mark.

2. To make a 15-inch pillow or hanging, enlarge the full color design by 300% on a photocopier (or select a single motif to use in other ways). Trace desired design from pattern page onto the canvas with the waterproof pen, or use pattern-page picture as a chart to work the design.

3. Staple canvas to assembled stretcher frame, if desired, making sure canvas is smooth and taut.

If you're working without a frame, do not fold your work. Instead, roll the work up around a cardboard tube, with the design inside, from the end you are not stitching, and hold in place with paper clips. Stitch dark colors before light colors, working with white last, so that fibers will not rub off on light yarn.

4. Cut yarn into 12-inch lengths. Separate strands of Persian yarn, using two strands throughout. Use the photos here and on the opposite page as color guides.

To save time, keep separate needles threaded with yarn of each color. Never carry thread across the back of your work for more than three or four stitches. Instead weave it through existing stitches or clip and start again in the new area. When starting first strand, leave 1 inch of yarn on back of canvas and cover it as you work.

5. Stitch pillow top: Work details first, from upper right-hand corner or color by color, then fill background. Work entire design in continental or basketweave stitch. See page 16 for stitch instructions.

6. Trim excess canvas around stitching, leaving ½-inch margins. Seal edges with clear nail polish. Block work by stretching and pinning in shape onto ironing board. Gently steam, holding iron above work. Allow work to dry completely before unpinning.

7. Cut velveteen pillow back same size as needlepoint pillow front.

8. Stitch pillow front and back together, wrong sides out, making ½-inch seams and leaving an opening in one side for turning.

The god's-eye appears here in this Sampler Pillow which also includes designs used by Indians from Arizona and New Mexico. The star in the upper left corner represents traditional Indian beadwork, and is separated from the Navajo god's-eye and feather design in the right corner by a vertical row of arrowheads. Below the star and to the left of a small god's-eye is a leaf-and-mountains design found on Pueblo pottery. The symbol in the lower right corner has been adapted from the Navajo Two Gray Hill rug design.

9. Turn pillow cover right side out; stuff firmly with fiberfill. Turn in raw edges ½ inch; slip-stitch opening closed.

Optional Trims:
1. If twisted-cord trim is desired, tack in place around edge of pillow.
2. Tassels are made from the 3-yard lengths of rust, tan and black yarns. Cut a piece of cardboard to the length of tassel desired. Wrap 3-yard lengths of yarn around cardboard 20 or more times, depending on thickness of yarn and plumpness of tassel required. Tie

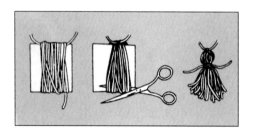

strands tightly around top, leaving at least 3-inch ends on ties; clip other end of strands. Wrap another piece of yarn tightly around strands a few times about 1 inch below top; tie and knot. Tack to corners of pillow.

Merry-Go-Round Motifs

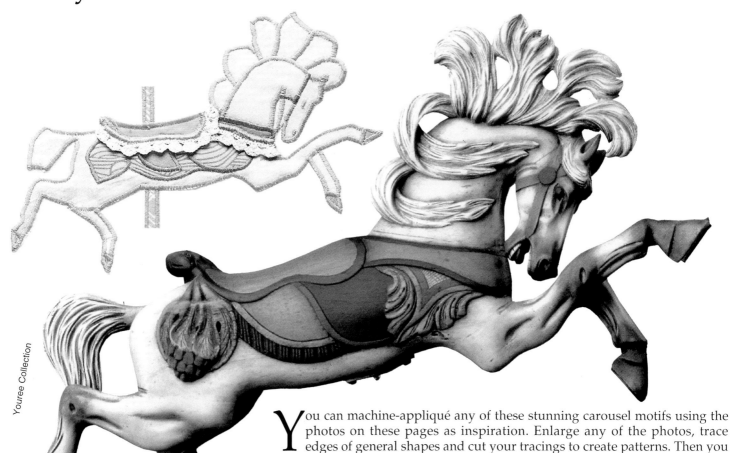

Youree Collection

You can machine-appliqué any of these stunning carousel motifs using the photos on these pages as inspiration. Enlarge any of the photos, trace edges of general shapes and cut your tracings to create patterns. Then you are ready to cut the pieces from fabric, planning the various layers of the design before machine-stitching in place.

Machine Appliqué

You may want to practice machine-appliqué techniques on scraps before starting the project. Refer to your sewing-machine instruction manual and set your machine for satin or appliqué stitch. Set the shortest stitch length (usually the length used for buttonholes or 24+ stitches per inch). Choose appropriate stitch width (you may wish to practice using widest setting). As you master machine-appliqué, you will adjust the stitch width as needed for the details of the project at hand. On some machines you will need to loosen the top tension by about half the normal setting to create a smooth stitch on top. Bobbin thread should not show on top.

Fabric for background (½ yard for single horse)
Small fabric scraps for appliqué
Fabric glue stick
Thread for machine-appliqué (choose colors to comple ment your fabric scraps)
Zigzag sewing machine; Notebook-weight paper

If your appliqué stitches pucker your work or if feeding fabric through machine is difficult, place notebook-weight paper underneath the background fabric and stitch through all thicknesses. The paper will tear away easily.

1. Cut background square to desired size. Carefully cut one each of pattern pieces.

2. Apply glue to fabric pieces with fabric glue stick and place pieces on background fabric using the diagram and photo as a guide. Piece numbers indicate placement order for best results.

3. Using appropriate colors, stitch over raw edges of fabric with machine-appliqué stitch.

4. Stitch details with appropriate widths and colors using diagram and photo as guides. Embellish your carousel horse with scraps of lace or other leftover trims you have on hand. Add them either by hand or slip edges under fabric pieces before you appliqué stitch.

Creative Cross-Stitch on Waste Canvas

Stevens Collection

Your cross-stitch animals can easily steal center stage on any smooth-surface, colorfast, washable clothing or purchased fabric item, like the sweatshirt shown here, the bib on an apron, a fabric carryall or diaper bag, or the ends of a table runner. Use your imagination and the cross-stitch motif of your choice and waste canvas, which may be purchased by the yard (it's 27 inches wide) at any needlecraft store. Waste canvas gives you an 8.5 count. (See page 68 for the cross-stitch chart for the motif shown above.)

The circa 1912 Coney Island steed above was carved by Marcus C. Illions. We interpreted it in cross-stitch as a black horse to be more dramatic and more versatile in its application to different background colors.

A single carousel horse called "Southern Belle," carved by Marcus Illions, sold for a record-breaking $101,000 at a late 1988 auction.

Both the rabbit, right, and fanciful "hippocampus" or sea horse, below, were carved by the Dentzel brothers in the Philadelphia style.

**Cross-stitch thread for project chosen
Purchased item that has an ample surface
   on which to work your motif
Waste canvas, cut to accommodate your
   motif with at least a 1" border**

Stevens Collection

1. Center waste canvas on the object on which you will be working. Baste around all sides and across center from upper right to lower left and upper left to lower right.

2. Following instructions for the cross-stitch project you have chosen, stitch through waste canvas and fabric item.

3. When pattern is completed, remove all basting threads. Dampen waste canvas with sponge or wet cloth. Wait 20 minutes, then carefully pull waste canvas away from fabric and stitched area strand by strand.

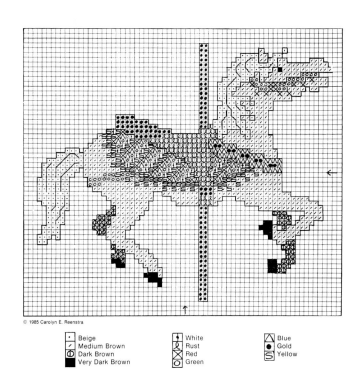

•	Beige	♦ White	△ Blue
∕	Medium Brown	✕ Rust	● Gold
Ⓓ	Dark Brown	□ Red	⑤ Yellow
■	Very Dark Brown	▽ Green	

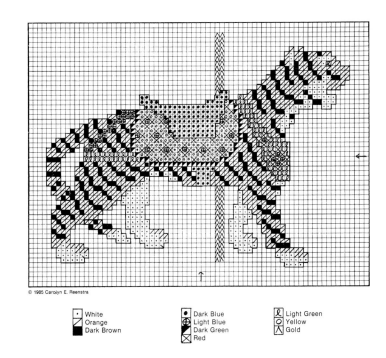

•	White	● Dark Blue	ℓ Light Green
▽	Orange	⊘ Light Blue	○ Yellow
■	Dark Brown	⊞ Dark Green	✕ Gold
		✕ Red	

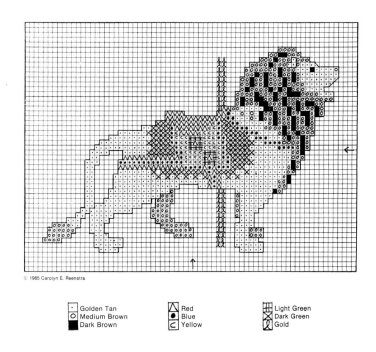

•	Golden Tan	△ Red	⊞ Light Green
○	Medium Brown	● Blue	✕ Dark Green
■	Dark Brown	C Yellow	▽ Gold

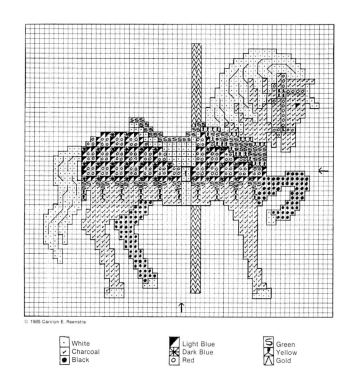

•	White	◣ Light Blue	⑤ Green
✓	Charcoal	✳ Dark Blue	✕ Yellow
●	Black	○ Red	△ Gold

*On
this page
we have interpreted
for cross-stitch the late 19th-century Coney-
Island-style carousel animals created by
Charles Looff, one
of America's most well-
known carousel
craftsmen.*

Cross-Stitch Carousel

*Charles
Looff is credited with
installing the first carousel at
New York's famous Coney Island
in 1876. He built his first three carousels
by himself before
opening a Brooklyn,
New York, carousel
factory.*

For all cross-stitch carousel animals:
**6-strand embroidery floss, 1 skein each
color, indicated on charts shown opposite**
**Aida cloth (14-count yields an image that is
about 5 by 3¾")**

Start stitching from center of design and
fabric. All single lines in any direction
indicate backstitching, not color. Use
two-ply floss for all stitches, except
where noted. Each motif uses the same
color symbols, but note that they represent different colors for each animal.

Stalking Tiger
When tiger is all stitched, backstitch
entire outline in one-ply brown. Also
backstitch outline of chest harness and
blanket, plus single stitches to indicate
toes, in one-ply brown.

To display your finished foursome,
frame each in gold and hang together
for a stunning wall grouping or
make each animal the center of atten-
tion on a pillow. Our Black Camelot
Steed has pranced onto page 67, where
you'll learn to use waste canvas, another way for your cross-stitch menagerie
to high-step into the limelight.

Brown Prancer
Yellow tassels on blanket are four-ply.
After horse is stitched, use one-ply of
the darkest brown to outline entire
horse, saddle, chest harness and all lines
in mane and tail, as indicated on chart.

Roaring Lion
After lion is completely worked, backstitch around entire outline in one-ply
medium brown. If you want the mane
and tip of tail to look more ragged (a
realistic touch to contrast with the
smoother outline), do not backstitch
around these sections.

Black Camelot Steed
All yellow tassels on blanket and harness buckles on head are four-ply floss.
When your horse is all stitched, backstitch a buckle in two-ply black on the
saddle strap. Using one-ply green, backstitch around each white stitch
in saddle. Use one-ply black to backstitch entire outline of horse and to
backstitch lines in mane and tail as
indicated on the chart.

Charts for Cross-Stitch

1. Use carbon paper to transfer your photocopy motif onto graph paper. Using a pen or dark-colored pencil, outline each block that encompasses the outline of your motif to create a jagged-edged rendering of your design. Next, outline all other important basic outlines in your motif in the same manner.

2. Use colored pencils to experiment with color combinations on your graph. Take your chart to a needlework shop, enlist the aid of the staff expert and choose your thread colors.

3. Once you are ready to work, define outlines with a backstitch, cross-stitch main areas as you would for any project and add detail stitches last. This will be an experimental, trial-and-error process. Be prepared to take stitches out if they don't look right or the color combination doesn't please your eye.

Both the magnificent horse (circa 1920) below and this beautifully carved goat (circa 1910) were done by Daniel Muller, who worked in the Dentzel brothers' Philadelphia factory. Muller is considered to have been the most talented of the Dentzel artists.

Abbott Collection

Daniel Collection

Charts for Knitting

Knitting charts are created in almost the same way. Graph paper designed specifically for knitting charts is available through knitting stores. Regular graph paper can be used, but the stitch-per-inch ratio may be a bit off.

1. Trace your properly sized motif onto the knitter's graph paper and experiment with color for your finished design. Enlist the aid of your knit-shop expert to choose yarns.

2. Check the stitch-per-inch ratio for the pattern of the item you want to make. Each square on your graph represents 1 inch. Multiply the number of stitches by the number of grid boxes and work your design row by row, changing yarn colors as necessary. Again, don't be afraid to tear out. Sometimes color combinations take on a look different from what you expect. It's easiest to remedy the problem as soon as you see it.

Stitching from Photos

Any of the carved figures parading through these pages may be resized and simplified to become templates, patterns or charts so you can recreate them in your chosen medium. On pages 66 through 69 you have seen how some of them look after we have converted them into appliqué patterns and cross-stitch charts. Any of these figures could also be traced onto fabric or paper, then painted, outline-stitched or filled in with crewel embroidery. You might even trace them onto a hard medium such as wood or a wall, then paint them in color using the original picture as a guide. If you choose to use any one or a combination of these figures in a nursery or playroom, for example, you might stencil a frieze of figures around the room at the top of the wall, then reduce them and stencil or paint them around a lamp shade. To make a nearly life-sized supergraphic painting on a wall you can photograph the printed picture with a 35-mm camera using slide film, then project the image on the wall to the desired enlargement, trace it lightly in pencil and paint it in with acrylics after taping around the outlines with masking tape. After resizing to fit, you could even trace the figures onto a sheet of wood, cardboard or Styrofoam, cut them out and paint them to make window-shade pulls or construct a mobile to hang over a crib. For resizing up to 11 by 17 inches, a photocopier is your best friend if you would like to turn a photo or piece of artwork into a motif for any medium. A printer or business-supply store will help you with this inexpensive process. You'll need the photo, book or artwork you wish to use plus the ideal measurements of the finished motif. The printer will determine how to enlarge or shrink down the image you supply to get a photocopy in the correct size for you to trace from. Remember that the vertical and horizontal dimensions of the original will increase or decrease proportionally when its size is changed.

The Philadelphia-style giraffe and cat shown here were created by Salvatore Cernigliaro, an Italian woodcarver who emigrated to America and went to work for the Dentzel brothers in 1903. Every Dentzel cat had something in its mouth— a bird, fish, frog or squid.

Abbott Collection

Stevens Collection

T his duck family is embroidered in the bright colors that children respond to. Mama duck is teaching her two little ones to get around in the water. As she instructs the duckling at her side, the other one leaps through the air in a daring dive that makes the cattails vibrate.

Darling Ducklings

Our finished picture measures 7½ by 10 inches when framed. Fabric measurements include a 3-inch allowance all around for fraying and framing. The design is embroidered entirely in cross-stitch. See page 15 for stitch diagrams. Also see pages 74 and 75 for a companion design (especially if you are fond of pink pigs).

6-strand embroidery floss in colors as noted at top of chart
Aida cloth (or other even-weave or even-weave-squared fabric that will give you 7 stitches per inch), 1 piece 14 by 16"
Embroidery needle

1. Work the design with two strands of embroidery floss. Mark center of fabric. Find the center of the chart.

2. Following the chart, begin work from the center and embroider back and forth across each color area. All bottom stitches should slant in one direction; all top stitches should slant the opposite way. As you work, catch loose ends under the embroidered stitches on the wrong side, and you won't have to weave them in later.

3. When you have completed one half of the embroidery, turn your work and the chart around and finish the picture in the opposite direction. See page 23 for blocking directions.

The finished picture can be framed (see pages 46 to 49) or made into a pillow or small hanging.

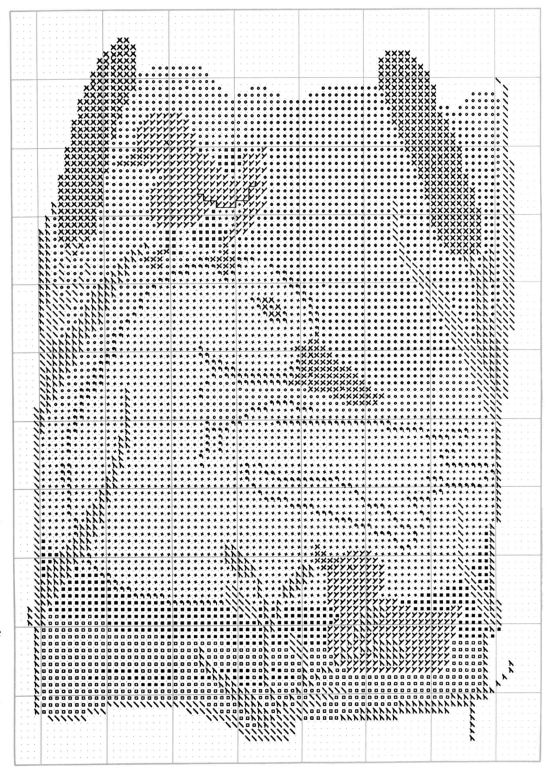

1 skein each: Light blue ▫ ▫ ▫   Medium pink ∘ ∘ ∘   Medium green \ \ \   Dark green ⟍ ⟍ ⟍

Medium blue ▪ ▪ ▪   Yellow ⟍⟍⟍   Red ● ● ●   Sienna ✕✕✕   White • • •   Gray ◗ ◗ ◗ Black ✗✗✗

<big>A</big> well-scrubbed, prize pink pig poses in his full majestic corpulence. His ears are pricked up in alert intelligence as if his attention has been

Appealing Piglets

drawn to a delicacy just beyond the picture plane. Around his neck a garland of appetizing apples glows as round and cheerfully as he.

This picture measures 7½ by 10 inches when framed. We have embroidered the design entirely in cross-stitch. See page 15 for stitch diagrams. For instructions and a companion cross-stitch design see pages 72 and 73. See page 23 for blocking directions.

6-strand embroidery floss, 1 skein each:

Light pink ○○○

Medium pink •○•

Dark pink ⊙○⊙

Olive green ▲▲▲

Medium light green \\\

Dark green ↘↘↘

Yellow ㄚㄚㄚ

White ✦✦✦

Gray ۹۹۹

Black ✕✕✕

Aida cloth, 1 piece 14 by 16"
Embroidery needle

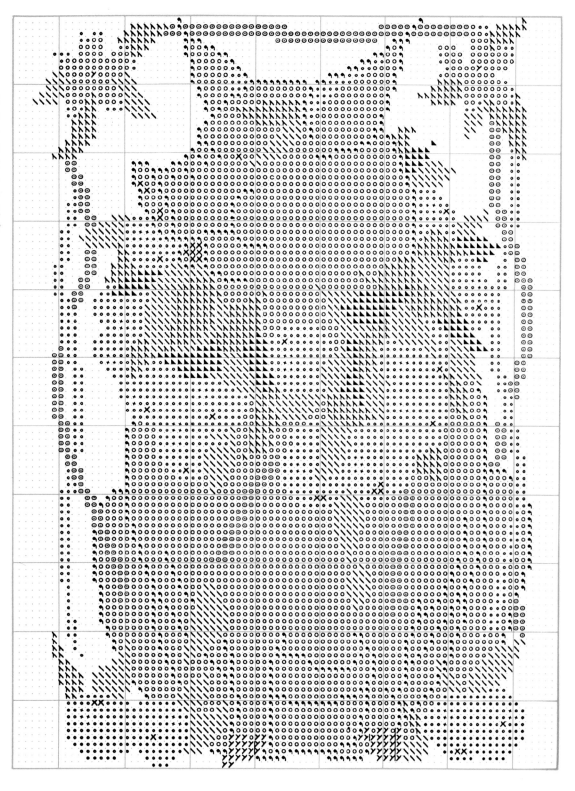

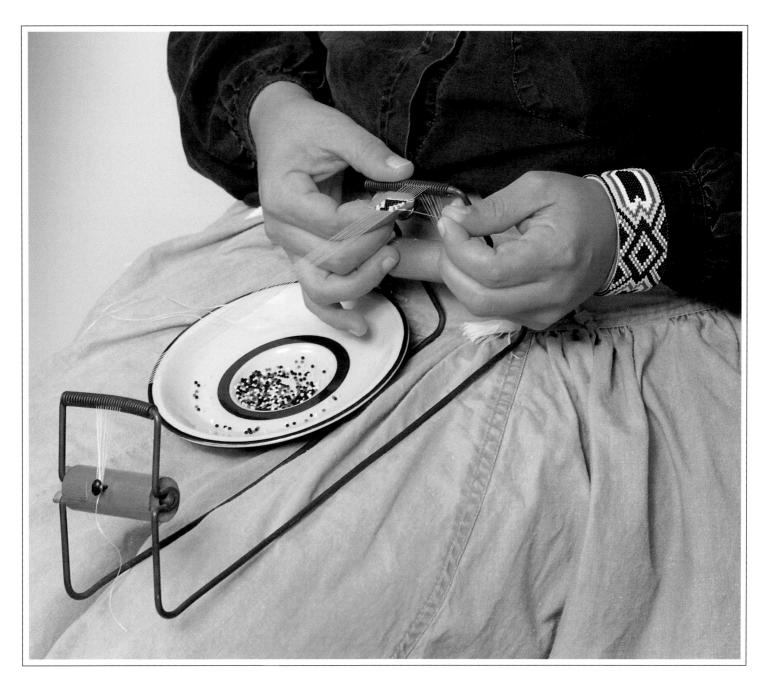

Wampanoag Bracelet

Before Europeans settled in New England in the 1600s, members of the Wampanoag tribe in Rhode Island and Massachusetts made decorative beadwork for ceremonial clothing from beads made of shells, wood, clay and stone. The English settlers introduced colored-glass beads to the New England tribe as a medium for trading. Wampanoag craftspeople still pass along the traditional methods of working with these colorful beads from parent to child. Alice Lopez worked the bracelet shown here on a simple loom sold in crafts shops. She selected the sacred colors of her tribe—red, yellow, black and white—which represent the four human races. Like other peoples whose beliefs have been shaped by living in cooperation with nature, Native Americans understand and accept its imperfections. That is why they always introduce a tiny flaw into their own handwork.

Materials for beading, including looms, beads, beading thread and needles, are available in most crafts shops. The pattern for the wristband opposite is on the pattern page. Once you have completed this simple piece, try designing your own belt, headband or decorative trim. A helpful rule to remember is: Always have an even number of loom threads and an uneven number of beads in each narrow row so that one vertical row of beads makes the center of the design.

Beading loom
Beading thread or nylon thread
Beading needle
One vial each red, yellow, black, white
    seed beads, size 12
Leather or heavy canvas, 2' square
Rubber cement
Sharp scissors; pencil; leather punch or awl

Stringing the Loom

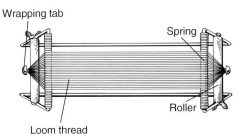

1. To string loom threads, tie the beading thread onto the wrapping tab at one end of the loom. Bring the thread over and between two springs, straight across the loom and over and between the opposite springs, then wrap once around the opposite wrapping tab. Continue to go back and forth until you have 22 loom threads on your loom. Wrap the end of the thread around the wrapping tab two or three times and tie in a knot to secure.

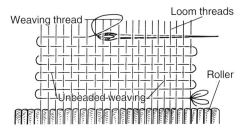

2. Thread the needle with about 3 feet of beading thread, single strand. This is your weaving thread. With one of the loom rollers facing you, tie the end of the weaving thread to the outside loom thread on the right. With the needle and thread, weave over and under the loom threads, working from right to left, then from left to right. Continue about 10 times back and forth, ending on top of the left outside loom thread.

Beading

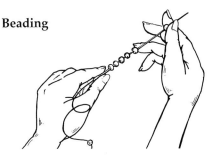

1. Reading the pattern from left to right, insert the needle through the hole in each bead; string the whole row of beads onto the weaving thread, matching the beads to the colors in the color guide accompanying the pattern.

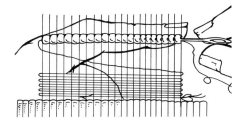

2. Bring the beaded weaving thread under the loom from left to right. Push beads up between each pair of loom threads as shown.

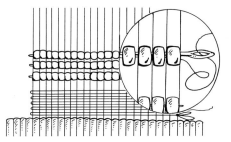

3. Holding beads above the loom threads, put the needle back through the beads from right to left. The needle must pass *over* the loom threads, and through the hole of each bead.

4. Work the rest of the pattern in the same manner. To finish, pass the weaving thread over and under the loom thread ten times as in step 2, Stringing the Loom. Tie the beading thread to the outside loom thread.

If you get down to about 4 inches of thread, bring the thread and needle back through the beads in the previous two rows; trim the thread. To start a new thread, string the needle again. Holding the end of the thread, pass the needle through the beads in the third row back, starting on the right side of the loom. Pass through second and first rows, ending on the left side. Trim the end and continue beading.

Making the Wristband

1. Cut the beadwork off the loom, including the unbeaded weaving at each end. Lay the beadwork on a piece of leather or heavy canvas. With a pencil, mark its width onto the leather. Add about 3 inches to the length of the beadwork and mark that dimension. Cut two pieces of leather this size.

2. Lay the beadwork in the center of the smooth side of one leather piece. Thread the beading needle with about 3 feet of single thread and tie a knot at the end. Tuck the unbeaded weaving underneath and bring the thread and needle up through the leather and between the first two rows of beads at one end. Bring the needle back down over one loom thread to tack the beading to the leather. Continue tacking about every five rows around the beadwork. Tack the other end in the same way and tie a knot in the thread on the leather side to secure.

3. Using rubber cement, glue the beaded piece of leather directly onto the rough side of the second piece of leather. Let dry 24 hours.

4. Use a leather punch or awl to pierce two holes about ¼ inch apart and ¼ inch in from one end. Wrap the band around your wrist, overlapping ends with the holes on the top. Put a pencil through the holes to mark the spots for the other two holes and punch them out.

5. Cut a leather thong ¼ inch by 6 inches. Align the two sets of holes and thread one end of the thong up through each set of holes. Tie knots at the ends of the thong, then tie it into a bowknot so the bracelet fits comfortably.

Dollhouse Rugs

Floor coverings are just as important in decorating your dollhouse or miniature room as they are in decorating your own home. They add the finished look that pulls a room and its furnishings together. Braided rugs and stenciled floor cloths are made much the same in miniature as they are in full size, except that the materials are scaled down to dollhouse size—yarn replaces wool fabric strips and muslin replaces heavy canvas. Hooked rugs are made from embroidery floss, using a method developed in Russia many centuries ago and brought here by immigrants. The original punch needles were made of bird wing bones and from quills, but now punch needles made of steel may be purchased from craft and needlework suppliers.

Hooked Rug

Tracing paper; carbon paper
Pair of tight-fitting embroidery hoops
White muslin large enough to fit in hoops
Punch needle, fitted with no. 1 needle
Embroidery floss for small rug: black, 3
　shades pink, 3 shades purple, 2 shades
　green, yellow; for large rug: dark brown,
　3 shades orange, 3 shades green, 3 shades
　rust or gold, black
White glue, thinned slightly with water
Small, sharp-pointed scissors

1. With tracing paper, trace outlines of patterns from the rugs in the photo, shown opposite. With carbon paper, trace rug patterns onto muslin; place muslin in hoops with pattern side up.

2. Thread needle with a single strand of floss about 36 inches long, in the darkest shade of one of the flower colors. Set the needle at a depth of 8 mm (5/16 inch).

3. Along the outline of a flower, punch needle straight down through muslin until handle hits squarely against fabric. Brace your hand on the hoop as if you were writing. Raise needle slowly just to surface of fabric—do not lift the point. Slide needle point across fabric, keeping eye of needle facing the hole just made, moving barely far enough to clear first stitch. Punch needle again through fabric and repeat this along pattern line to outline flower. Stitches should be about 1 mm (just less than 1/16 inch) apart.

4. Continue making stitches, following inside this outline row and keeping rows close together. After a few rows, switch to the middle shade of floss, then to lightest for center of flower petals.

Until you are used to the feel of the needle, check the reverse side of your work frequently to be sure the loops are of the same length and are close enough together to form a compact hooked appearance. The reverse side will be the finished rug surface.

5. To change thread colors, slip free end close to surface of fabric and begin a new color. Do not tie knots in floss. When design areas are finished, fill in background color to edge of rug.

6. Remove from hoops and cut fabric, leaving 1/2 inch around the edge of rug. Clip fabric carefully just to edge of rug at 1/2- to 3/4-inch intervals. From the edge

scraps, cut a muslin backing 1/4 inch smaller than rug.

7. Lay rug face down on a flat surface and spread glue around outer edges. Fold muslin flaps back tightly, pressing in place with fingers. Be sure muslin does not show from front of rug. Spread glue on remaining part of rug and place muslin backing over rug. Press in place and allow rug to dry thoroughly. When dry, press with a warm iron if rug does not lie perfectly flat.

Stenciled Floor Cloth

Heavyweight unbleached muslin or thin
　artist's canvas
Gesso
Brush for gesso
Clear satin spray varnish
Sharp-bladed scissors
Small stencil in border pattern
Acrylic stencil paint
Small stencil brush
Iron and pressing cloth
Pencil

1. Cut muslin 1 inch larger than dimensions of finished floor cloth. Coat one side lightly with gesso and allow to dry. Repeat on other side.

2. Spray lightly with varnish, allow to dry and repeat on other side.

3. Carefully cut fabric to size of finished floor cloth. Be sure edges are perfectly straight and evenly cut, since this is the finished edge.

4. Mark the center of each edge lightly in pencil and, working from these marks outward to the corners, mark placement of stencils. Make sure design fits evenly and borders are even on all sides. It is important to plan your placement before you begin stenciling to be sure design is evenly spaced.

5. Stencil designs. Allow to dry thoroughly and erase all pencil marks. Press lightly with a warm iron, protecting surface with pressing cloth.

Braided Rug

Cotton rug yarn in desired colors
Sewing thread and straight pins
Needleworker's scissors
Thin nonwoven interfacing
White glue, thinned slightly with water
Waxed paper

1. Cut three strands of yarn, 24, 22 and 20 inches long. Tie these together at one end by wrapping tightly with a strand of sewing thread and tying securely.

2. Braid the three strands evenly, but not too tightly, always pulling the left-hand strand a bit tighter than the others to make a slight curve in the braid.

3. When you have braided a few inches, lay the braid on a flat surface and carefully form a flat coil, tucking the beginning of the braid underneath. Pin in place with straight pins and continue braiding. By forming the rug as you braid, you can see how big the rug is and where you want to change colors.

4. To change colors or add more yarn, tie a very tight square knot and clip the loose ends close to the knot. When you braid it in, be sure the knot is hidden in the braid. By making the yarn strands different lengths, you avoid having two knots making a lump in the finished braid.

5. When the rug is the desired size, tie the end of the braid by wrapping in thread as you did at the beginning. Tuck this under the edge of the rug and pin in place. Cut the yarn.

6. Cut a circle of interfacing 1/8 inch smaller than the finished rug. Straighten the pinned coils so the braid is perfectly even and lay it upside down on a flat surface.

7. Spread a thin layer of thinned glue on the back of the rug and lay the interfacing circle over it. Press in place with fingers. Turn over and lay rug on a sheet of waxed paper. Carefully remove pins and adjust braid so it lies flat and even. Allow to dry thoroughly. Press with an iron when dry if the rug does not lie perfectly flat.

Fancy Boxes

The art of tatting has been passed down from generation to generation in my family, each generation teaching the next. My mother remembers watching her grandmother, my great grandmother, tatting. A family diary describes how my ancestors tatted to pass the time as they walked behind covered wagons during the long journey halfway across the country to Iowa.

Many cherished gifts have been tatted and exchanged in our family over the years. One of my favorites is a Tatted Fancy Box. It can be round, like the ones my great grandmother brought from Ireland, or heart-shaped, like the ones shown here. Fill them with potpourri, favorite pieces of jewelry, hair ribbons or any number of other tiny treasures.

—Kathie Ballard

You may make a larger or a smaller fancy box, simply by changing the size of thread you use. See pages 82 and 83 for general tatting instructions and abbreviations.

1 ball ecru thread: cotton Knit-Cro-Sheen (for small size) or Speed-Cro-Sheen (for large size)
Tatting shuttle with hook for joining, or shuttle and crochet hook
Fabric stiffener
Clear acrylic spray
Optional for lining: ¼ yard fabric (polyester, velour and polyester-cotton blend work well); 1 yard fusible bonding web
Extra-thick tacky glue
1 yard ribbon, in desired color, ¼" wide (for small size) or ⅜" wide (for large size)
3 ribbon roses, ¼" (for small size) or ⅜" (for large size)
Yarn needle
2 to 4 oz potpourri
Netting or fine lace (to wrap potpourri in)

Bottom of Box, Cloverleaf Center

Wind shuttle with thread, leaving ball attached.

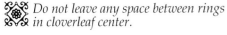 *Do not leave any space between rings in cloverleaf center.*

R of 4ds, 5p sep by 4ds, 4ds, cl r. 2nd r, 4ds, join in last p of 1st r, 4ds, 6p sep by 4ds, 4ds, cl r. 3rd r, 4ds, join to last p of 2nd r, 4ds, 4p sep by 4ds, 4ds, cl r. Rw, ch of 4ds, 5p sep by 4ds, 4ds, rw, r of 4ds, p, 4ds, join to 3rd p of 1st r, 4ds, p, 4ds, cl r, rw, ch of 4ds, 3p sep by 4ds, 4ds, rw, r of 4ds, p, 4ds, skip last free p on 1st r, join to 1st free p on 2nd r, 4ds, p, 4ds, cl r, rw. Ch of 4ds, 3p sep by

4ds, 4ds, rw, r of 4ds, p, 4ds, skip 1p, join to bottom p of 2nd r, 4ds, p, 4ds, cl r, rw, ch of 4ds, 2p sep by 4ds, 4ds, rw, r of 4ds, p, 4ds, join in same p on bottom of 2nd r, 4ds, p, 4ds, cl r, rw, ch of 4ds, 3p sep by 4ds, 4ds, rw, r of 4ds, p, 4ds, join to last free p of 2nd r, 4ds, p, 4ds, cl r, rw, ch of 4ds, 3p sep by 4ds, 4ds, rw, r of 4ds, p, 4ds, skip 1p, join to 3rd p of 3rd r, 4ds, p, 4ds, cl r, rw, ch of 4ds, 5p sep by 4ds, 4ds, join at beginning of work, cut and tie threads.

Sides of Box

Tie ball and shuttle threads together, r of 4ds, p, 4ds, join to 1st p of 1st ch on bottom of box, 4ds, join to next p, 4ds, p, 4ds, cl r, rw, ch of 4ds, 2p sep by 4ds, 4ds, rw. * R of 4ds, p, 4ds, join to next p, 4ds, join to next p, 4ds, p, 4ds, cl r, rw, ch of 4ds, 2p sep by 4ds, 4ds, rw *, repeat between *'s 10 more times to go around bottom of box, join to last ch at top of 1st r. Cut and tie threads.

Top of Box

Same as bottom, but do not cut and tie threads. Continue on to last round for ruffled trim. Last round of top: ch of 4ds, p, 4ds, skip 1p, join to 2nd p, continue ch of * 4ds, p, 4ds, join in next p * around top of box, repeating between *'s skipping last p, join at starting point. Cut and tie threads.

Finishing

1. Stiffen box bottom and top with fabric stiffener, shaping both pieces and reshaping again when halfway dry. When dry, spray with acrylic sealer.

2. If you want to line your box, fuse wrong sides of lining fabric together with fusible web, according to directions on web. Using the box bottom as a pattern, cut linings for bottom and top from fused lining fabric. Spread tacky glue on inside of top and bottom, then press linings in place.

3. Box lids may be left loose or hinged. To hinge, sew together top and sides of box at curved places on either side of top hearts with Knit-Cro-Sheen thread and yarn needle.

4. Use ribbon to tie bows, saving some ribbon to tie potpourri bag with. Glue ribbon roses and bows to top of box as desired.

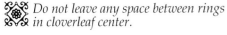 *To fill your box with potpourri, place potpourri in center of net or lace, gather up and tie with remaining ribbon. If necessary, trim to fit, then place in box.*

This antique German silver shuttle is 3¾ inches long. In the center of the decorative incising there is an oval space for the owner's initials. Tatting encourages conversation (in Italian, the word for tatting is almost the same as the word for gossiping) because, like crochet and knitting, it is a repetitive task with variations that produce patterns. With practice, fingers fly. Why, then, decorate a tool flying so fast one can hardly see it at work? Perhaps the decoration honors the tool rather than its owner. As the skill of an artist grows so does the artist's gratitude toward the tool that faithfully translated his or her skill into a thing of beauty.

A form of knotting, tatting is a cousin of macrame, lace making and netting. Its origins are thought to lie in seamen's knots. Tatting is based on one (and only one) of them, the *simple half hitch*, worked in pairs. The half hitch has its practical origins as a knot that could be tied in opposing pairs along a second rope which had both ends secured, as on a moored boat.

By varying the thread, the tension, the spacing and the direction of these pairs of half hitches, delicate lacy patterns can be created in almost infinite variety.

Reading a Pattern

Some abbreviations for tatting instructions are the same as those used in knitting, but a few are different.

* —repeat pattern between asterisks
ch—chain (a length not pulled up to make a ring; made from ball thread)
cl r—close ring
ds—double stitch
p—picot
r—ring (made from shuttle thread)
rw—reverse work
sep—separated (to indicate separation, by knots, between picots)
sp—space (no knots are worked on the thread, as space is left to create a picot; space will vary in length according to pattern directions)

No. 20 cotton thread, smooth and slightly twisted; if tatting thread is not available, use crochet cotton
22" piece no. 20 cotton thread, blue or desired color
Tatting shuttle, either new metal or antique ivory (the only difference is that some of the newer ones have removable bobbins that are faster to wind, and some have a tiny hook on one end that is handy for joining; if your new shuttle is plastic, be sure it has a point)

Half Hitch

Before beginning to tat, use this simple trick to help you understand the principle. Using plain string and your fingers, make two loose half hitches onto a second piece of string, the "working line." Now pull sharply on the looped string, relaxing the working line, and you will see the knots reverse. The working line has become the knotting string and the former knotting string is now straight. Tatting is nothing more than making those same knots with thread, using a shuttle.

Tatting Techniques

Preparing to Tat

1. Wind thread on shuttle, leaving about 12 inches free.

2. Tie blue thread to free end of shuttle thread with a square knot. Pull knot tight and clip short ends.

3. Hold knot between thumb and tip of first finger of your left hand, with blue end away from you and white end toward you.

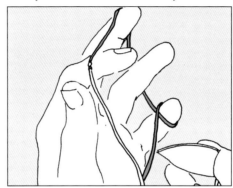

4. Put blue end over middle and ring fingers and wrap its tail a few times around your little finger. Curl this finger in against your palm to anchor thread. Try wiggling your second finger back and forth and you will see the blue thread tighten and loosen. That is how you control tension.

5. Hold shuttle like a pencil in your right hand, with thread coming off *back* side of it (the side away from you). Catch this thread behind your right middle and ring fingers to give the shuttle thread some tension control. You will always hold the shuttle in your right hand and it will be your working thread. The blue thread is the one you tie knots onto (later reversing them), and the area you work in is the space of about 2 inches, held between point where you grasp knot and middle finger. Later, when you are working on a project, there will be no knot. It is only to tie together the two colors used in learning.

To Make the Basic Knot

The basic knot is made in two parts like a double half hitch (clove hitch) knot. The difference between this and other knotting is that after you make each half hitch, you reverse its direction by pulling the working thread tight. This forces the thread on which you made the knot to reverse places, becoming the knotting thread.

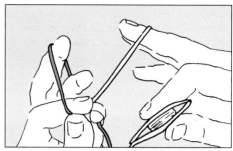

1. Bring white thread (shuttle) under your index finger and up over the middle finger of your left hand.

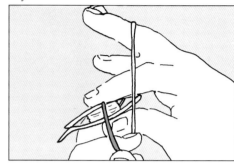

2. Put shuttle (either end) under both white and blue threads, heading to left.

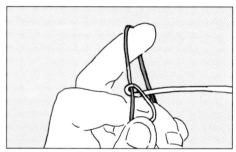

3. Without turning shuttle, bring it back *over* blue, but under white. This makes a loop which you should tighten gently until it lies close to blue thread and about an inch from your thumb.

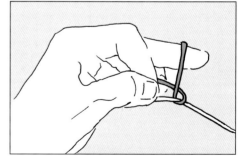

4. *To reverse the knot,* relax left middle finger to loosen blue thread and pull white thread with a slight snap. This should reverse knots **(rw)**. Move this knot up close to knot under your thumb. This is first of the half of the pair of knots.

5. *To make other half,* work in same direction, putting shuttle *under* white and *over* blue and returning it under blue and over white. When you return, shuttle must be below (toward your thumb) thread you just put through or you will get a twist instead of a loop. If your thread is coming out the back of the shuttle, this will happen almost automatically. If your shuttle is turned over, it is nearly impossible to do this correctly.

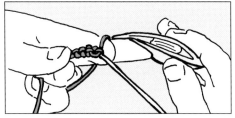

A completed chain of double stitches.

6. Snap this knot to reverse threads and move it in close to first. This completes a double stitch *(ds).*

Everything else in tatting is done with these basic knots. A picot is simply a space between two pairs of stitches. When these are moved along the thread, the connecting space of thread forms a loop.

When picots and knots lie in a straight row along a continuous thread, they are called a chain *(ch).* When this is pulled to form a circle, it is called a ring *(r).*

Once you have the idea of how to make the knots and snap them to reverse the threads, you are ready to abandon the blue thread and work on one continuous thread. For a small project you can cut off a length and wind it on the shuttle, or you can leave the ball of cotton on the free end. For larger projects, always leave the ball attached.

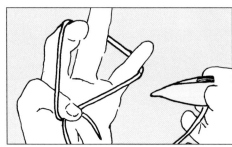

In making a ring, the thread is held somewhat differently in the left hand. Grasp the shuttle thread between the thumb and index finger, the free end toward you, and wrap it completely around your other three fingers, then back between your thumb and index finger to form a full circle. The working area and the method of making the knots remain exactly the same.

To Make Picots and Rings

1. Work four double stitches (sets of knots).

2. Make first half of another double stitch, but as you slide it back into position under your thumb, stop about ¼ inch from preceding stitch. Complete second half of the stitch.

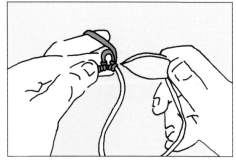

3. Slide entire stitch close to previous double stitches. The little loop formed by space in thread is a picot.

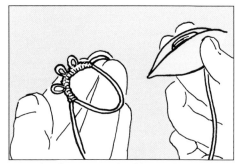

4. Make three more double stitches and another picot. Repeat this for a third picot.

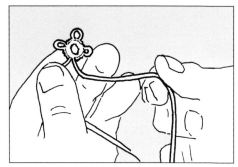

5. Make four double stitches. Holding these securely between thumb and index finger of left hand, draw shuttle thread tight so first and last stitches meet and pull chain into a ring. This is called closing a ring *(cl r).*

6. Make four more double stitches ½ inch away from this ring.

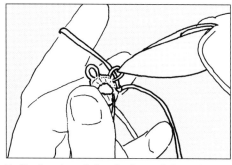

7. Push point of shuttle through last picot made in ring just completed, and nudge a little loop from the thread which you are holding around fingers of your left hand back through the ring.

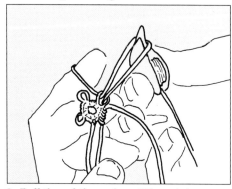

8. Pull thread through until loop is large enough to pass shuttle through. Draw shuttle through loop and pull shuttle thread tight.

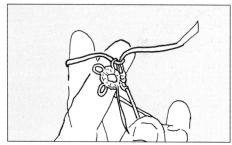

9. Carefully raise left middle finger to tighten circle thread and join new ring to old one. This also makes first half of next double stitch.

10. Complete this stitch and continue to form another ring.

Beginners have difficulty keeping the thread running freely through the knots. The only way to be sure of this at first is to test each knot after it is snapped into place. If one stitch is not reversed properly, the thread won't draw. Since there is no way to undo knots once formed, there is no remedy but to begin again.

Italian Stuffed-Work

In 18th-century Florence, ladies-in-waiting in the courts of powerful princes devoted much of their time to decorative needle painting. In one technique, called *trapunto*, they added subtle colors to stitched shapes of sheer fabric by stuffing the shapes with colored yarns. They used sheer silks, batistes and organdies for the top layer so the colors of the yarns beneath would show. In old pieces, the oat-meal texture of the coarsely woven muslin commonly used for backing often shows through the sheer top. We have applied the art of trapunto to a Victorian picture frame in which the padded pastels create an elegant yet romantic effect. The design of grapes, leaves and tendrils has been adapted from a decorative valance around the top of George Washington's canopied bed displayed at Mount Vernon, Virginia.

Unlike quilting, where the entire piece is padded and quilted, trapunto highlights only the design in relief. The top photo detail, right, reveals the muslin backing with snipped ends of colored yarns that have been stuffed into the stitched shapes between the muslin backing and the batiste front. Another form of trapunto, in which no color shows through, employs two opaque fabrics, which allows for the use of cotton or polyester batting to stuff large areas. Counterpane (also called *stuffed quilting*) and cord quilting, which uses string instead of yarn, achieve similar effects.

Two 12 by 14" pieces of sheer white batiste
12 by 14" piece coarsely woven muslin
Iron, to transfer design on bound-in sheet
10" embroidery hoop
White cotton quilting thread and needle
Green embroidery thread
20" pieces of purple, green and yellow 3-strand soft wool rug yarn
Blunt wool needle; bodkin or toothpick
White basting thread; needle; pins
Two white mats to fit 8 by 10" frame with precut 5 by 7" oval and cardboard backing
Glue gun; sewing machine
Two 8½ by 10½" pieces of white cotton sheeting (for frame back)
Double-folded white bias tape
6" strip of self-sticking white Velcro
Double-sided paper tape
Photograph and easel (optional)

Marking the Fabric

1. Loosely baste together edges of one piece each of batiste and muslin so grains of fabric run in the same direction.

2. Use the oval opening of the mat board to mark where the opening will be on the muslin. Iron motif (see large, bound-in pattern sheet provided) onto the back of the muslin. Iron the design on the upper right corner, around the oval. It will be in the upper left after it is stitched.

Stitching and Stuffing the Design

1. Stretch design in embroidery hoop. With white quilting thread, use a running backstitch to outline the designs. Stitch along both sides of the tendrils with green embroidery thread.

2. Separate the three-strand rug yarn into single or double strands as noted below. Work on the muslin side, using a blunt wool needle. For the vines, draw a single strand of green yarn between the rows of stitches. Fill out the shape without breaking the batiste threads. Trim yarn ends.

3. Pull a double strand of green yarn through the leaves, working from the center of the leaf outward. Trim yarn ends. Draw a double strand of yellow yarn through the bow design, pulling the needle out of the muslin at the corners. Trim yarn ends.

4. Use a sharp needle to separate the threads on one side of a grape to make a small hole for the blunt needle to enter. Thread the blunt needle with a single strand of purple yarn. Draw it through the hole and out the other side of the grape. Trim yarn, with ¼-inch piece on either side. Use the bodkin to pack the yarn end back through the entry hole so the shape is round without overstuffing. Trim yarn ends. Repeat for each grape.

Assembling the Frame

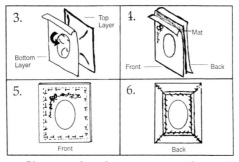

1. Glue together the two mats with precut ovals to make a stiff double layer.

2. Lay remaining piece of batiste flat. Position work on top with oval tracing up and edges aligned. Pin all layers together at corners. Pin around oval 1 inch outside tracing. Machine-stitch with white thread following oval tracing.

3. Cut fabric out of oval leaving ⅛-inch inside seam. Clip curves. Pull top layer of batiste through oval hole. Iron seam flat around oval on the back.

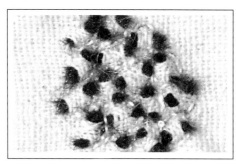

Stuff colored yarns into stitched designs between the muslin backing and the sheer batiste top, as shown here for the grapes.

4. With one hand, hold work right side up on top of precut oval mat. With other hand, pull bottom layer of batiste through oval hole in mat to back. Also pull trimmed seam allowance to back.

5. Pull edges of fabric tightly together around outside of mat to stretch out wrinkles and puckers. Pin together at four corners and along edges. Stitch around four sides ⅛ inch outside pins.

6. Trim excess fabric, leaving ¼-inch seam allowance. Pin, baste and stitch double-folded bias tape along edges. Pull loose fabric tight around back of frame on all four sides. Whipstitch as you go.

Frame Back

1. Lay cardboard backing on top of two layers of sheeting. Trace around edges with pencil. Stitch layers together along tracing, leaving top open. Trim, leaving ¼-inch seam allowance. Slip backing in. Fold trimmed edge in; slip-stitch closed.

2. Fasten front of frame to back with 1-inch strips of Velcro placed inside the four corners and centered on sides. Reinforce self-sticking adhesive with glue. Affix double-sided tape to back of photo; put photo in place, attach back and easel.

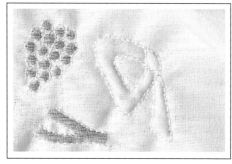

The sheer batiste top allows the colors of rug yarns stuffed beneath to show through.

Guest Towel

Around 40 years ago, a young Swedish-American schoolgirl made the yellow towel above for her teacher. The teacher's granddaughter admired the embroidery on the towel every time she visited her grandmother's Minnesota home. Just recently, the grown-up granddaughter embroidered a brand new huck towel, above right, for her grandmother—a reminder of those special childhood visits.

Huck toweling (also known as *huckaback*) is a natural for its own style of embroidery, often referred to as *Swedish weaving*. If you look closely at the huck toweling, you'll see a series of double threads woven on the face of the fabric in even, staggered rows. These double threads are the *hucks* and are perfect for running embroidery threads, or *catch threads*, through them. The exact spacing makes the work easy as well: You need only count hucks and skip back and forth from row to row to make the zigzag and dovetail patterns used in the towel on the right.

Originality is the essence of this particular needle art and patterns are seldom employed. Getting started is as simple as finding a piece of huck toweling, some floss and a needle. Begin by making a sampler using the stitches shown opposite. Once you know the stitches, decorate a tea towel, apron or pinafore with your own colorful Swedish weaving.

Huck toweling is available at most fabric shops. Since it is 100% cotton, wash and dry the fabric to preshrink.

Use as many strands of floss as you like—all six will make a bold design, three a more delicate one.

At the end of each row, hide and secure floss ends by running them back through and beneath the last few hucks worked. Cut floss close to work. If the piece you are embroidering is part of a garment, it's not necessary to hide ends; they'll be caught and hidden in seams.

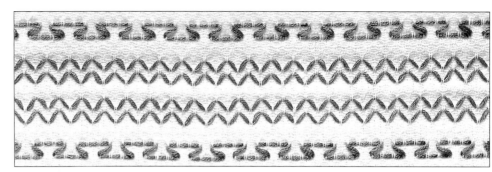

If you are making a pinafore or apron from a purchased pattern, substitute huck toweling for the waistband and add some pretty Swedish weaving.

Embroidered Tea Towel

⅔ yard huck toweling
Straight pin
6-strand embroidery floss: 1 skein each of 3 colors (we used rust, gold and blue)
No. 24 tapestry or embroidery needle

A blunt tapestry needle will keep the needle from penetrating the fabric by mistake.

1. Fold toweling in half lengthwise and find center row of hucks. Mark with a straight pin near edge of towel.

2. Cut 1½-yard piece of one color embroidery floss. Using desired number of strands, thread into needle. Beginning in center, 3 to 4 inches from edge, insert needle through a pair of hucks. Pull through about half of the embroidery floss; allow the other half to hang free.

3. Working from center to one selvage, make a large running zigzag, 10 hucks from peak to peak, across towel. At selvage, run thread back through last few hucks, then cut close to work.

4. Thread needle with remaining half of floss and work other half of row, repeating step 3. Hide ends.

5. With color 2, work another row of large zigzags, beginning one huck to right or left of first row, following an identical path. Hide ends.

6. With color 3, work another row of large zigzags to right or left of second row, as in step 5. Hide ends.

At the peak of each zigzag you can weave over and under embroidery rows to achieve an effect more like weaving. Many hucks will be shared by two colors of floss.

7. Work two more rows, each to the right or left of the last row, using color 1. Hide ends. Repeat with color 2. Repeat with color 3.

8. For last row, using color 3, work large zigzag in opposite direction of other rows (see photo, opposite).

9. One huck above and below the band of large zigzags, work a row of dovetails. Each dovetail is six hucks at its widest part. Start in center of the fabric and work to edges so design will be centered.

10. Fringe ½ inch of towel on each end to finish.

Pinafore or Apron Waistband

Purchased pattern for pinafore or apron
Prewashed huck toweling (for amount see step 1)
2 straight pins
No. 24 tapestry or embroidery needle
6-strand embroidery floss: 1 skein each of 2 colors

1. See purchased pattern for width and height of waistband, including seam allowances. Cut a piece of huck toweling to this size, being sure that hucks are running vertically. Find horizontal and vertical centers of fabric and mark with straight pins.

2. Thread needle with desired number of strands of color 1. Beginning one huck below vertical center and directly in horizontal center, pull half of thread through, leaving other half hanging free. Work small zigzag (one huck peak to peak) from center to one edge. Do not hide ends. Return needle to center and complete row.

3. Run another row of zigzags the same size one huck below the first row.

4. Three hucks below the last row, run a row of dovetails, again starting in center and working toward edges. Work in color 2, making four hucks wide.

5. Two hucks above the zigzag rows, work another zigzag row in color 1 the same size but opposite in direction to other zigzags, as shown in photo above. One huck above this row, work another identical to it.

6. Three hucks above last row, work a row of dovetails in color 2, as in step 4. Waistband is ready to be inserted into garment, following instructions on purchased pattern.

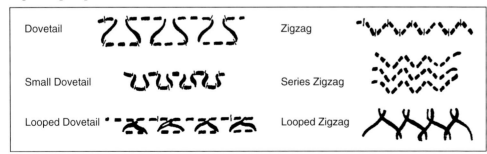

Dovetail		Zigzag	
Small Dovetail		Series Zigzag	
Looped Dovetail		Looped Zigzag	

Here are just two basic Swedish weaving stitches and several of their variations. Change thickness, color and stitch combinations to create your own patterns or follow the instructions above to create our patterns.

T he doll named Sara is riding in a 1904 wicker car- riage with a parasol attached. Her owner has more dolls, each with its own nameplate. When she

Perambulator Nameplate

returns home, her cross- stitch baby buggy bumper banner will become a vanity plate to be hung on the end of her crib. The idea works just as well for real children.

Two branches, embroidered in magenta and blue-green, form the borders of this design. The child's name is embroidered in the center, in yellow capital letters. The hanging is edged with cotton cord piping and backed with felt.

The finished nameplate measures about 10½ by 3¾ inches. Fabric measurements include a 1½-inch seam allowance. The design is embroidered in cross-stitch. If you need more explicit instruction, see page 15. See pages 20 to 22 for a cross-stitch alphabet chart.

13½ by 6¾" piece of even-weave linen or other fabric, with about 18 threads per inch, in white or desired color
6-strand embroidery floss, 1 skein each of blue-green, magenta and yellow, or desired colors
30" piece of premade cotton cord piping in white or desired color
13½ by 8" piece of felt (for backing) in white or desired color
Cotton sewing thread to match fabric
Graph paper

Embroidering the Border
1. Use four strands of embroidery floss throughout. Find, then mark, center of fabric. Following the chart, work the border design as shown, beginning at midpoint of lower edge. The embroidery should extend to 1¾ inches from the raw edges.
2. Turn work around, return to starting point on chart and fabric, and repeat the design in the opposite direction.

Embroidering the Name
1. Refer to a small charted alphabet from pages 20 to 22. Sketch out on graph paper the child's name so that it will fit onto the central space of fabric within the embroidered border. Each square of the graph represents a cross-stitch space. Each embroidered cross-stitch covers 2 by 2 threads of fabric.
2. Count the number of threads your design will cover horizontally and vertically, and draw placement lines on the fabric with a soft pencil. Embroider.

Blue-green **YYY**   Magenta **⊘⊘⊘**

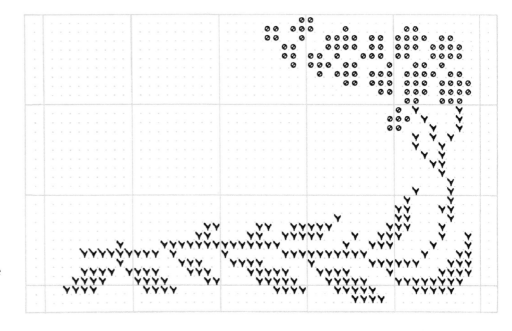

Assembling the Hanging
1. Position piping around edges of right side of embroidered fabric, slightly rounding corners of the square. Piped edge should be facing in and piping seam line should lie on the fabric seam-allowance line. Machine-baste ¼ inch above seam line.

2. Lay backing felt over the piping and fabric, matching lower and side edges, right sides together. Stitch around three sides, leaving top open. Clip corners and trim seam allowance to ½ inch. Turn right side out.

3. Extend the felt out from the top edge, and make two vertical cuts from felt edge to piping to narrow the flap about ¾ inch on either side. Fold the flap over toward the back and tuck the end inside. Trim and tuck inside excess felt on either side of flap. Topstitch all around hanging between piping and linen.

Napkin Rings

It was not so long ago that a silver napkin ring with engraved initials was an appropriate gift for a newborn. For adults the memory of them occupies a treasured place in their recollections of early childhood. Often a napkin ring was passed down to a namesake. Such gracious traditions can be preserved by making rings of wood and fabric and decorating them with paint or cross-stitched initials. Party idea: Put each guest's name or initials on a ring. These will act as place cards and party favors, too.

Painted Wooden Rings

Materials needed for all styles:
Unfinished wooden napkin rings (available in crafts shops)
Acrylic paints; acrylic finish
½" brush for basecoating
Medium-fine sandpaper

To prepare all styles for decorating: Sand the wood smooth. Paint on a basecoat with the color suggested in individual instructions or to suit your own taste. Let dry. Apply a second basecoat.

Posy Ring

Apply acrylic basecoat, as described above. Use **acrylic fabric Paintwriters** to apply a motif. See the full-size pattern for our posy motif and color suggestions. Spray with acrylic finish.

Cookie-Cutter Ring

Flat **wooden cutouts** like the heart are available at crafts shops, or use cookie cutters as patterns and cut out your own. Pick a different cutout for each family member or use the heart motif on the pattern page.

1. Apply a basecoat to the napkin ring and heart or other cutout as described above and consult pattern page for floral design and color suggestions.
2. Apply paint with a sponge to make a border around outside of the cutout. Create flower centers and petals by applying paint with the handle end of a **no. 0 short liner brush**. Paint the stems and leaves using the brush end. Add filler dots to the design with the handle end of the brush. Let dry.
3. Glue cutout to the napkin ring with a **glue gun or craft glue**. Spray with acrylic finish.

Sitting-Pretty Ring

Browse through crafts and second-hand shops for tiny knickknacks to top a wooden ring. Unpainted **bisque figures** like our bird are readily available in crafts shops.

1. Basecoat the napkin ring. Sponge a border around the edges of the ring. Using a **no. 0 short liner brush**, paint a "comma stroke" design around the center of the ring (see the pattern page for motif and color suggestions).
2. Use a **no. 6 square brush** to paint a wash of acrylic which has been thinned with water to add color to your figure.
3. Add details with a **no. 0 liner.** Use a **glue gun or craft glue** to glue **dried baby's breath** onto the napkin ring to form a nest for your figure. Let dry.
4. Glue figure onto the nest. Spray with acrylic finish.

Cross-Stitch Monograms

We've provided two colorful cross-stitch motifs to embellish monograms. Refer to the cross-stitch alphabets on pages 20 to 22. Each ring is a **7-inch length of 14-count ivory Ribband**.

Heart/balloon motif

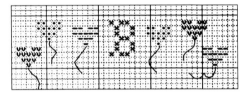

Flower Thread colors: X 210   — 415
                          V 310   • 525

1. Use the color guides and charts shown here to choose your **cotton embroidery thread** colors and work your design: We used one strand to work the flower motif and two strands for the heart/balloon motif. Center the initial or initials and work them first.
2. To finish, press a ¼-inch seam to the wrong side of each end. Overlap ends; hemstitch with desired color embroidery thread to close the ring.

Fabric Napkin Rings

Fabric and other sewing scraps like ribbon, lace and piping cord and Velcro are about all you need to make these washable, versatile napkin rings.

Ribbon and Lace Napkin Ring

1. Using any combination of **fabric, lace, ribbon, ruffled lace or embroidered trim**, cut 6-inch pieces and layer as desired.
2. Fuse to **stiff iron-on interfacing** and stitch where necessary to hold pieces together. Sew a small patch of **Velcro** to the center back of one side of strip. Sew another piece of Velcro to the right side of the other end of the strip so that you can form a ring by pressing the Velcro patches together.

Braided Napkin Ring

Cover **three 8-inch pieces of piping cord** (any size you like) with **fabric**. Sew ends together and braid. Form a ring and stitch ends to finish.

Pieced Napkin Ring

1. Interface a **7- by 2-inch pieced strip** with **stiff iron-on interfacing**.
2. Cut a **7- by 2-inch lining** from a matching fabric scrap. With right sides together, sew lining to pieced strip using ¼-inch seams on three sides.
3. Turn right side out and stitch the open end closed. Press and stitch ends together to form a ring.

Flower motif

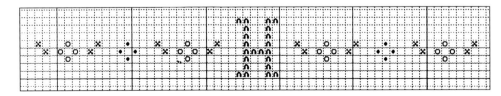

Flower Thread colors: X 445   O 296
                          ∧ 550   • 260

Bolsters & Pillows

The bolsters shown above are decorated with either cross-stitch or drawn-thread embroidery on even-weave linen or other fabric. Even-weave fabric has the same number of threads per inch lengthwise as crosswise. The weave of the fabric must be fairly coarse, so that the threads can be counted precisely in order to duplicate the design. You only need to know or learn four of the easiest embroidery stitches—satin stitch, four-sided stitch, cross-stitch and backstitch.

Stuff bolsters either with loose stuffing, such as fiberfill, or with prefabricated foam shapes. A drawn-thread pillow must be interlined to prevent the stuffing from showing or escaping through the holes if loose stuffing is used. If a prefabricated pillow is used, the interlining is optional and heavier fabric is necessary only for the bolster ends. Fabric measurements include a very deep seam allowance of 1½ inches. This allows for fraying of edges during embroidery and makes basting unnecessary.

Interlinings, backings and side pieces should be made with materials of firmer weave. We used muslin and broadcloth in colors to match the linen. Fabrics of different colors or finishes will produce different effects. Openwork can be emphasized by lining the embroidery with a darker color. The side pieces of a bolster or the backing of a pillow can be made of shiny woven silk or satin that picks up the color in the embroidery threads.

Please refer to pages 14, 15, 18 and 19 for diagrams of embroidery stitches and other supplementary information. Directions for all pillows shown above follow.

Floral Bolster

The finished product measures 16 inches long and 12 inches around. The seam allowance is 1½ inches.

15 by 19" piece even-weave linen or other fabric, about 18 threads per inch, pink or desired color

15 by 25" piece fabric of similar or firmer weave for interlining and end pieces (or 6 by 9" piece if using a prefabricated insert)

26" of preruffled eyelet trim, 2½" wide

Size 8 pearl cotton: 2 skeins white or desired color

6-strand embroidery floss: 2 skeins white or desired color

Cotton sewing thread to match fabric

Polyester fiberfill or prefabricated bolster 16" long and 12" around

Embroidery needle

Drawn-Thread Bolster

The finished bolster measures 11 inches long and 10 inches around.

13 by 14" piece coarse, even-weave linen or other fabric, about 12 threads per inch, off-white or desired color

13 by 20" piece broadcloth for lining, interlining and end pieces (or a 6 by 9" piece if using a prefabricated bolster)

24" preruffled eyelet trim, 2½" wide

Size 5 pearl cotton: 1¾-oz ball off-white or color to match fabric

6-strand embroidery floss: 2 skeins off-white or desired color

Cotton sewing thread to match fabric

Polyester fiberfill or prefabricated bolster, 11" long and 10" around

Embroidery needle

Geometric Bolster

Finished bolster measures 12 inches long and 10 inches in circumference.

13 by 15" piece even-weave linen or other fabric, about 18 threads per inch, pink or desired color

13 by 22" piece interlining fabric (or a 7 by 10" piece if using a prefabricated insert)

24" preruffled eyelet trim, 2½" wide

Size 8 pearl cotton: 1 skein white or desired color

6-strand embroidery floss: 1 skein each dark blue and light blue, or desired colors

Cotton sewing thread to match fabrics

Polyester fiberfill or prefabricated bolster, 12" long and 10" around

Embroidery needle

Four-sided stitch ▢▢▢   Satin stitch |||≡|||

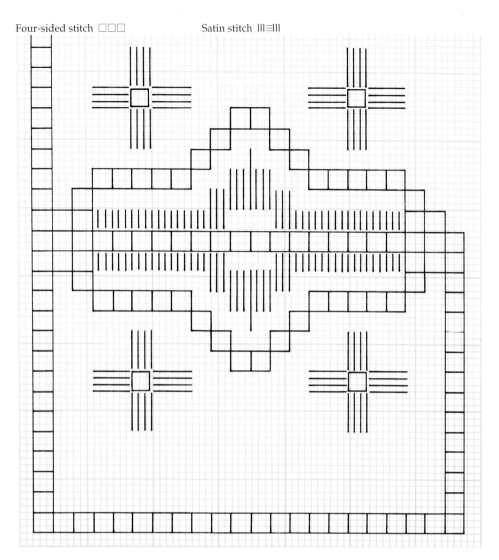

Chart for Floral Bolster: Blue lines represent the individual threads of woven fabric. Black lines indicate embroidered stitches. Squares represent four-sided stitch; close-grouped parallel lines indicate satin stitch. Each four-sided stitch is three threads square and each satin stitch extends over four threads. Count threads carefully. The Floral Bolster is shown on the far left in the photograph opposite.

Cutting and Embroidering

1. Use a double strand of pearl cotton for the four-sided stitch and a double strand of embroidery thread for the satin stitch. Embroider stitches consistently in one direction. Satin stitch should be worked either from left to right or from right to left. Four-sided stitch can be embroidered either horizontally or vertically. Work in the manner most comfortable to you. Give each stitch, particularly the four-sided stitch, a tug to group and separate the threads of fabric and create an openwork effect.

2. Cut two pieces of fabric to sizes given in materials list, one of linen and one of interlining material. You will need a strip 6 by 9 inches (7 by 10 inches for the Geometric Bolster) left over for end pieces.

Drawn-Thread Bolster

Joining the Ruffle

1. Pin eyelet ruffle to the right side of the embroidered linen along the two side edges, right side down, with the ruffled edge facing in and the other edge of the ruffle extending slightly past the seam allowance. Turn seam allowance under and press so that ruffle extends outward from fabric edge. Machine baste along seam allowance.

2. Turn the unruffled edges of the linen, and all four edges of the interlining, under 1½ inches and press. Place linen and interlining together with right sides out and machine-stitch close to edge of fabric. (If you have no interlining, follow this step without it.) Remove basting threads.

3. Hand stitch the unruffled edges together to form a cylinder and stuff. Fold ends of ruffle around each other and hand stitch.

To Work the Floral Bolster:

1. Mark center of fabric. To make pattern symmetrical, begin embroidery halfway along one side edge and work toward lower edge, keeping embroidery about ½ inch inside seam allowance, 2 inches from raw edges. Turn work and complete design in opposite direction to mirror first half.

2. Repeat design along opposite side edge. Establish the framework of four-sided stitches first and then fill in satin-stitch motifs.

To Work the Drawn-Thread Bolster:

Mark center of fabric. Following the embroidery chart, you can either work the border of a single row of four-sided stitches first and then fill in the horizontal alternating rows of satin stitch and four-sided stitch, or work the horizontal rows first and surround them with the border. Embroidery should extend to about ½ inch from the seam allowance (2 inches from raw edge). There should be three threads separating each four-sided-stitch row from each satin-stitch row.

To Work the Geometric Bolster:

1. Following the embroidery chart, establish the framework of four-sided stitches first, making a double row of squares along the two side edges.

2. Work an open-cornered square of satin stitch just inside each square of four-sided stitch. Alternate light-blue squares with dark-blue squares.

3. Embroider a little rectangle of five satin stitches at the center of each square. Alternate light-blue centers with dark-blue centers.

Four-sided stitch (double strand) □□□   Satin stitch (single strand) |||≡|||

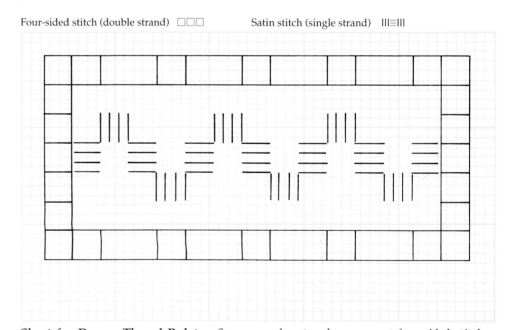

Chart for Drawn-Thread Bolster: *Squares and rectangles represent four-sided stitch. Parallel lines indicate satin stitch. Blue lines represent the threads of the woven fabric. Black lines indicate the embroidered stitches. Note that the horizontal rows of four-sided stitch are made up of short stitches that wrap around three threads of fabric and long stitches that wrap around six threads. The vertical stitches are all short, while the horizontal stitches are alternately long and short, with two short stitches at each end. The vertical rows of four-sided stitch that run along the side edges are comprised only of short stitches.*

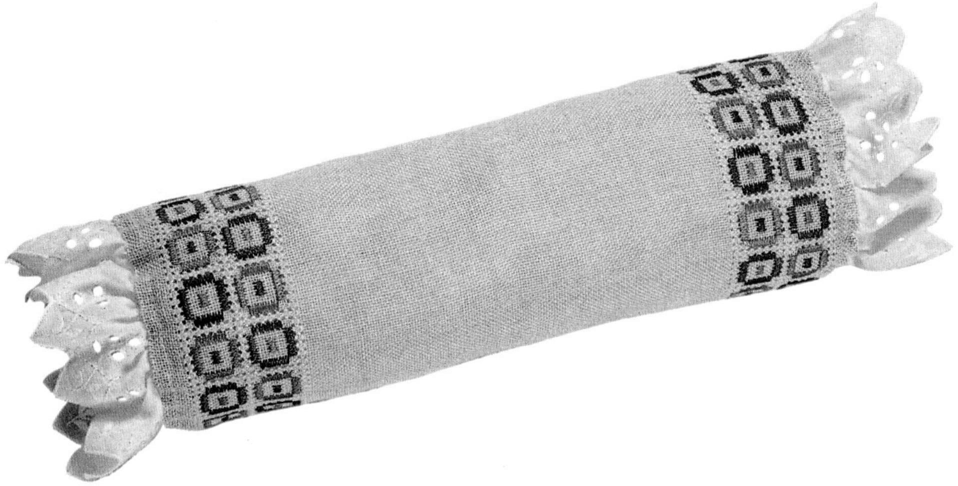

Geometric Bolster

Making and Joining the End Pieces

For either the Floral or Drawn-Thread Bolster, cut out two circles with 4¼-inch diameters for end pieces. For the Geometric Bolster, cut out two circles with 4¾-inch diameters for end pieces.

Clip and turn edges under ½ inch. Machine-stitch close to edge. Hand-stitch circles to each end.

Four-sided stitch □□□

Satin stitch |||≡|||

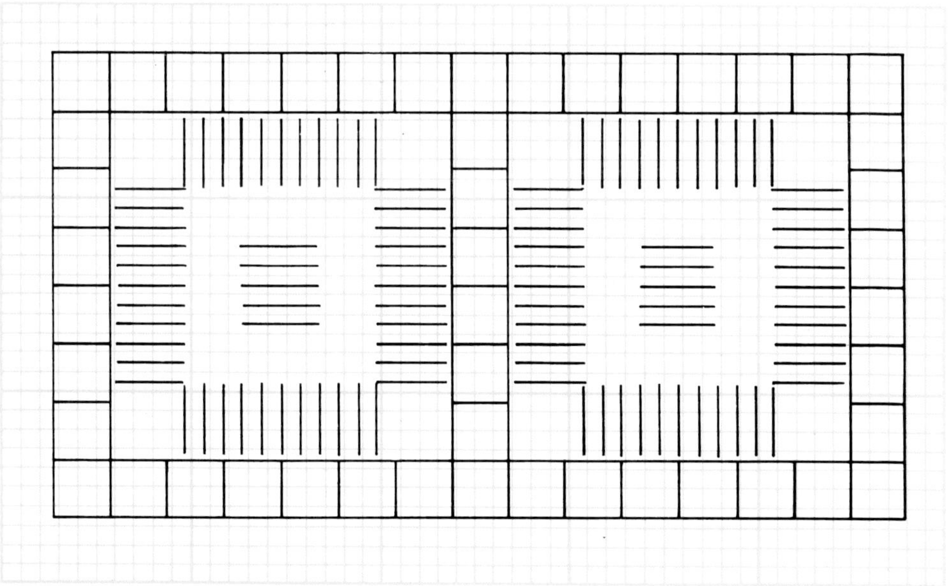

Chart for Geometric Bolster: *Blue lines represent the individual threads of woven fabric. Black lines indicate embroidered stitches. Squares represent four-sided stitch; close-grouped parallel lines indicate satin stitch. Each four-sided stitch is three threads square and each satin stitch extends over four threads. Count threads carefully.*

Heart Pillow

The finished pillow measures 7 inches across at the widest point and 6 inches down the center of the heart, excluding the ruffle. Pattern measurements include a 1½-inch seam allowance.

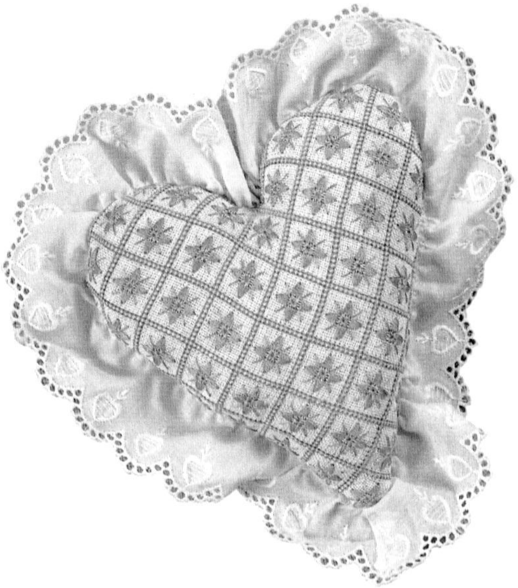

11 by 11" piece even-weave linen or other fabric, about 18 threads per inch, off-white or desired color
11 by 22" piece fabric similar or firmer weave for backing and interlining (if you are using a prefabricated pillow insert, interlining is optional and you will need only a 12 by 12" piece for backing)
28" of preruffled eyelet trim, 2½" wide
6-strand embroidery floss, 2 skeins green or desired color
Cotton sewing thread to match fabric
Polyester fiberfill or prefabricated pillow insert of the correct dimensions
Embroidery needle
Water-soluble marking pen

Marking the Fabric

Decide whether you want the embroidered design to run straight up and down on the pillow or diagonally (the pillow shown is embroidered diagonally). Enlarge the pattern of the heart (on page 96) by 200% using a photocopying machine. Place enlarged pattern on the fold of the linen, with arrow along straight grain of fabric. Trace heart and seam allowance onto the linen only with water-soluble pen. Do not cut out.

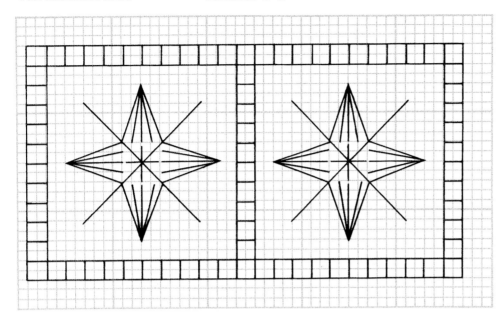

Chart for Heart Pillow: Blue lines represent individual threads of woven fabric. Black lines indicate embroidered stitches. Count threads carefully. Each four-sided stitch is two threads square. Each square of fabric enclosed by four-sided stitch is 20 threads square. The points of the four big flower petals extend to within two threads of the edges of the square.

Embroidering the Design

Use two strands of embroidery floss throughout. Embroider your stitches consistently in one direction—satin stitch either from right to left, or left to right; four-sided stitch either horizontally or vertically. Work in the manner most comfortable to you. Extend all embroidery slightly beyond the seam allowance.

1. Embroider the grid of four-sided stitches. The grid divides the fabric into 20-thread squares.

2. Embroider a satin-stitch flower in the center of each square.

Putting the Pillow Together

1. Pin three layers of fabric together—the embroidered linen, the interlining and the backing, with the linen on top, embroidered side up. Cut out the heart through all three layers.

2. Machine-baste interlining to wrong side of linen, ½ inch from edge (if you don't have an interlining, proceed without it).

3. Pin eyelet ruffle to right side of embroidery, with ruffled edge facing in, and other edge of ruffle extending slightly past seam allowance. Overlap ends of ruffle ½ inch and trim excess. Turn ends under ¼ inch and fold them around each other. Machine-stitch ruffle to fabric directly on seam allowance.

4. Position backing fabric over embroidered fabric, right sides together. Pin and sew seam directly over previous stitching line, leaving an opening for turning and stuffing (if you are using fiberfill, 2 or 3 inches is sufficient; if you are using a prefabricated pillow, a larger opening is necessary).

5. Clip and trim seams. Turn the pillow right side out and stuff. Hand stitch opening closed and sew ends of the ruffle together.

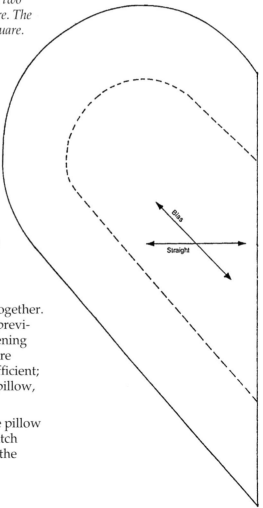

Floral Pillow

Even-weave linen or other fabric with about 24 threads per inch, 1 piece 13 by 13" in white or desired color

Fabric of similar or firmer weave for the interlining and backing, 1 piece 26 by 13" (if using a prefabricated pillow insert for stuffing, the interlining is optional and you will need only 1 piece 13 by 13" for the backing)

44" preruffled eyelet trim, 2½" wide

6-strand embroidery floss, 1 skein each: light pink, medium pink, olive green, medium light green, and white (if you are changing colors, you will need 1 skein each: 2 shades of one color for the flower tops, 2 shades of another for stems and leaves, 1 of a third color for the borders)

Cotton sewing thread to match the fabric

Embroidery needle

Polyester fiberfill or prefabricated pillow insert, 10 by 10" square

Embroider all your stitches consistently in one direction: satin stitch, backstitch and cross-stitch either from the right to left or from the left to right. Take care that in cross-stitch your bottom stitches all slant one way and your top stitches slant the opposite way throughout the work. Work the four-sided stitch either horizontally or vertically, whichever is the more comfortable for you. Use four strands of embroidery floss for the drawn-thread stitches and three for the cross-stitch and backstitch.

Cutting

Cut three pieces of fabric, 13 by 13 inches; one piece of linen for embroidering, one interlining and one backing (unless you are using a prefabricated pillow insert; then you only need to cut the backing; the interlining would be optional).

Embroidery

Review the embroidery chart (on page 98) before attempting to start the work. Following the chart, work from the borders toward the center.

1. Work the double row of adjacent four-sided stitches all along the border, then the double row of satin stitches.

2. Work the short diagonal of 3 four-sided stitches that extend from each corner of the pillow, and the four-sided stitch above and between each group of satin stitches.

3. Embroider the squares of four-sided and satin stitches within each corner of the finished border.

4. Center four clusters of flowers in cross-stitch and backstitch between the little squares and extending a little way beyond them. (Refer to the pattern chart on page 98 for the flower clusters and their location relative to the border corner design.)

Assembling the Pillow

1. Machine baste the interlining to the wrong side of the linen, ½ inch from the edge. (If you aren't using an interlining, go directly to next step.)

2. Pin the eyelet ruffle to the right side of the embroidered fabric, right side down, with the ruffled edge facing toward the center and the selvage edge extending slightly past the seam allowance. Overlap ends of the ruffle ½ inch and trim the excess. Turn ends under ¼ inch and fold them around each other. Machine-stitch the ruffle to the fabric directly on the seam allowance.

3. Position backing fabric over embroidered fabric, right sides together. Pin and sew seam directly over previous stitching line, leaving an opening for turning and stuffing. (A 2- to 3-inch opening is sufficient, if you are using polyester fiberfill; a larger opening will be necessary if you are using a prefabricated pillow insert.) Clip and trim seams.

4. Turn pillow right side out and stuff. Hand stitch the opening closed. Sew the ends of the ruffle together. Wait for the compliments to start.

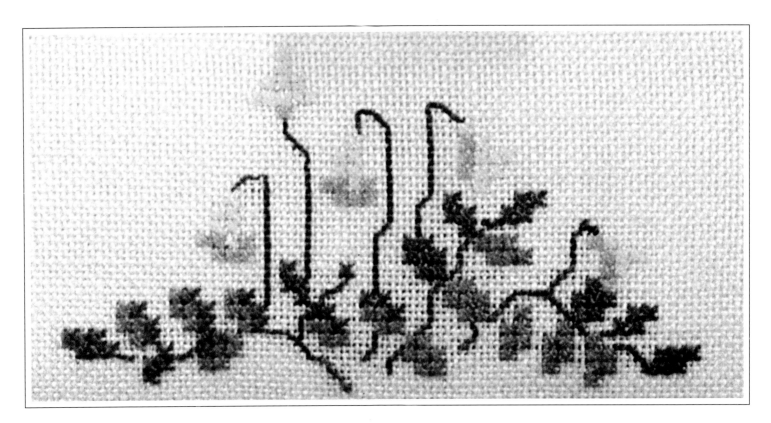

Light pink cross-stitch	ooo			
Medium pink cross-stitch	₀₀₀	Medium light green cross-stitch	— —	Satin stitch
Olive green cross-stitch	➤➤➤	Olive green backstitch	---	Four-sided stitch

Light pink cross-stitch ooo
Medium pink cross-stitch ooo
Olive green cross-stitch ➤➤➤
Medium light green cross-stitch — —
Olive green backstitch ---
Satin stitch ☐☐☐
Four-sided stitch ⫼≡⫼

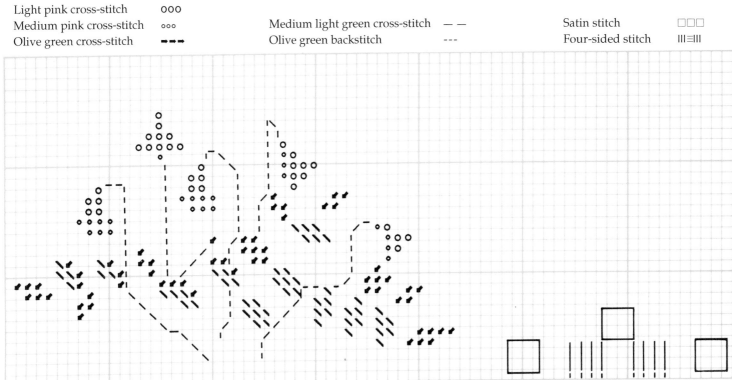

After establishing the border and corner motifs, embroider the flowers. A portion of one corner motif is reproduced in this chart to show you where to place the flowers. The broken lines that form the flower stems are worked in backstitch. All other symbols represent cross-stitch, a different symbol for each color. Unlike drawn-thread work, these stitches are intended to cover the surface of the fabric and should be worked with a fairly slack tension.

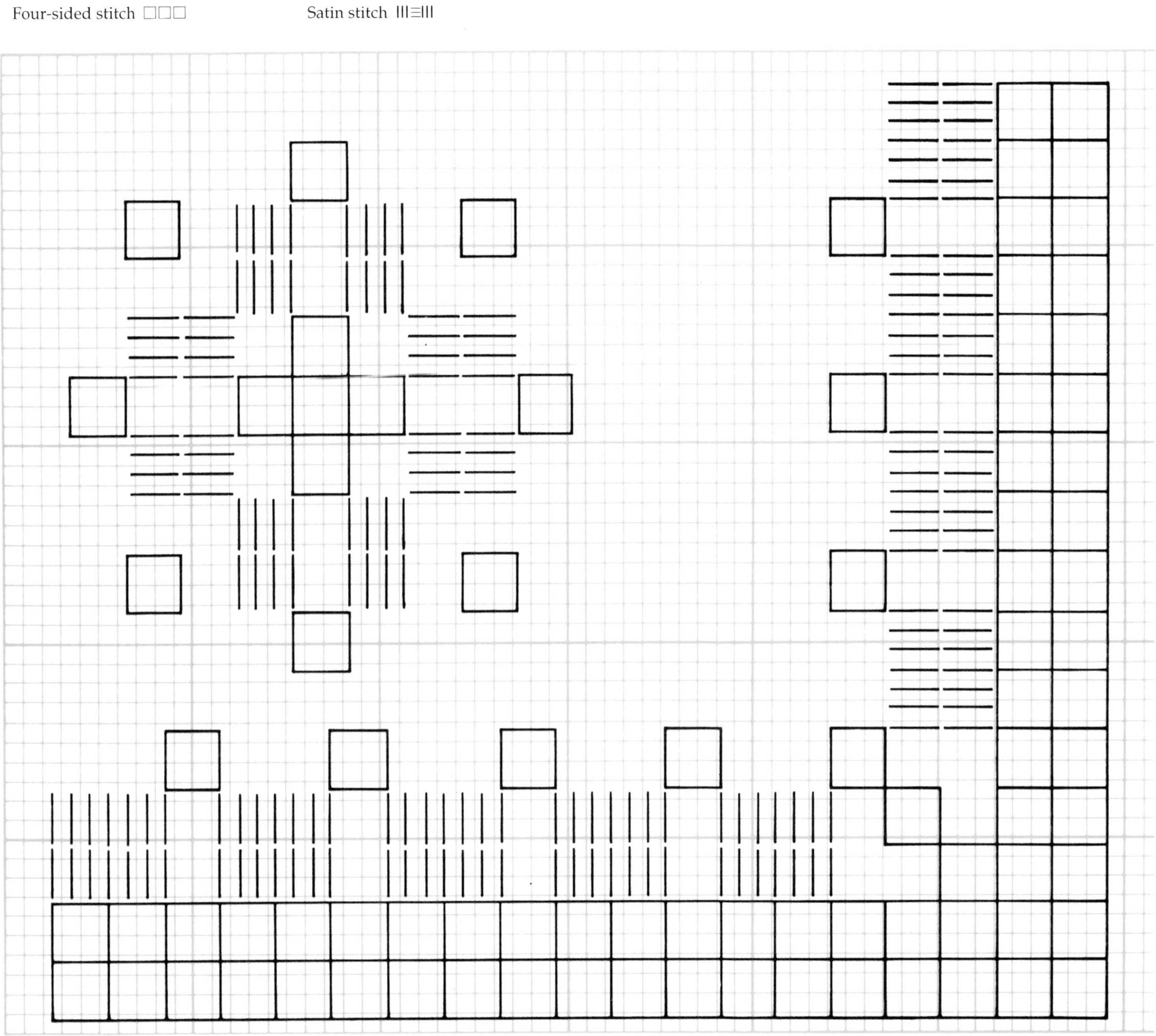

Four-sided stitch ☐☐☐   Satin stitch III≡III

Chart for Floral Pillow: *Shown here is the pattern of drawn-thread embroidery, which forms the border of the pillow, and the square motif, which is repeated in each corner of the border. Blue lines represent individual threads of woven fabric. Black lines indicate embroidered stitches. Each square is a four-sided stitch and each* *lone vertical is a satin stitch. Give each stitch a tug as you make it to group some threads of the fabric together and separate others. This creates the open-work pattern of holes that is characteristic of drawn-thread work.*

Teddy Bear Boutique

If you have a fondness for fuzzies, herein you'll find projects for people of all ages to use to wear, hug and decorate their dens. Our pinafore is made from a purchased sewing pattern in white cotton piqué. Directions for working the embroidery stitches may be found on pages 14 and 15.

Goldilocks' Pinafore

BABY BEAR

MAMA BEAR

PAPA BEAR

3. Adding 1 to 2 inches of fabric around edges of pieces, trace pockets and bib, including embroidery outlines, to piqué fabric. Cut one bib piece and two 5½- by 6-inch pockets from white cotton fabric for linings.

4. Insert piece to be embroidered in hoop and stitch in the colors and stitches indicated on pattern. Use two strands of floss for stripes of Papa Bear's pants and Baby Bear's shirt and for flower petals. For waistbands, hatbands, Baby Bear's tie and Mama Bear's collar, fill in areas with rows of backstitches made with three strands of floss.

5. Use outline stitch for bears' bodies; use three strands of light-brown floss. With one strand of light-brown floss, stitch tiny lines of fur approximating lines indicated on pattern. Fill in eyes and nose with satin stitches and dark-brown thread. Backstitch mouths with pink thread. Follow key for other stitches. Use backstitch unless otherwise indicated.

6. Line the embroidered pockets and bib with the cotton fabric before attaching them to the pinafore.

7. Assemble pinafore according to purchased pattern instructions. Trim pinafore with rickrack and ruffled eyelet, if desired.

Pattern for pinafore
White piqué, yardage given on pattern plus additional ¼ yard for pockets
½ yard white cotton fabric for bib and pocket linings
Light-pink and light-blue rickrack (optional); white ruffled eyelet (optional)
Dressmaker's carbon paper
Ruler
Embroidery floss (DMC numbers): 1 skein each light brown (840), green (3347), blue (809), pink (605), rose (603), yellow (445), light green (996) and gray (414); 1 yard dark brown (433)
Embroidery hoop and needle

1. Cut pinafore pieces from piqué using purchased pattern. From full-size patterns on this page, trace Baby Bear embroidery design to center of bib pattern within seam allowance; omit tiny lines of fur.

2. Make a pattern for pockets 5 by 5½ inches long; add 1½ inches to top and ½-inch seam allowance to sides and lower edges. Trace Mama Bear and Papa Bear to center of pockets about 1 inch from bottom edge and ½ inch above seam line; again, omit tiny lines of fur.

Key to Stitches

1	Outline
2	Straight
3	Lazy daisy
4	French knot

It is a known fact that teddy bears are capable of feeling every emotion known to humans, perhaps some others, too. Every bear has a special look that expresses his or her character, and you may decide that the bear you make should have a unique sort of expression. When you have stuffed your new bear and are about to add the fea-

Bear-Faced Features

tures to its face, look at the head shape or slope of the shoulders for hints on how it feels about life. You might think "Oh, she's so serious" or "He looks like he's just waiting to get into trouble." These pages tell you a little about how to form each part of the face so it contributes to the personality your bear will have.

Mouth

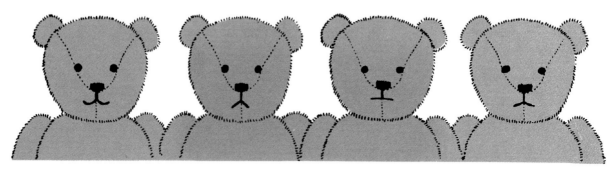

Happy Smile   Needs Friend   Stubborn   Serene

Like people, teddy bears have very expressive mouths. The traditional teddy bear mouth is an upside-down Y shape. The expression of the mouth is determined by the length and the angle of the stitches that form the slanted branches of the Y. To experiment with different mouth expressions, cut two small pieces of yarn and pin them on the face along the lines of the mouth. On a traditional, no-nonsense bear, the mouth slants downward in two straight lines. To make a wide-open smile, place the lines straight sideways. If they slant upward the bear may look silly. You may also leave slack in the stitches to form a curve, which may make him or her look warm-hearted but perhaps a bit formal, even shy. If the fur doesn't hold the curve of the yarn in position, take a few overcast stitches, using black thread, to tuck it in place.

Ears

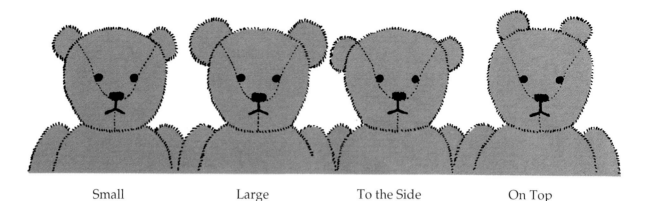

Small   Large   To the Side   On Top

The ears are a very distinctive part of a bear's anatomy. Their size and shape should be in keeping with the bear's character. For example, a staid, serious bear wouldn't look right with big floppy ears. Since the ear pattern is a simple shape, you should feel confident enough to do a bit of your own pattern making. You can draw ears that are a bit larger or smaller, or ears that are curved differently. If you like, test several ear shapes by cutting up some of the scraps of fur. Then try pinning the ears on in different positions and at different angles.

Nose

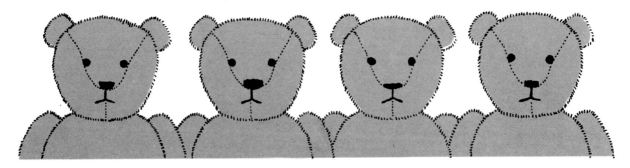

Triangle   Large Oval   Flat Oval   Small Oval

The nose may not be a bear's most expressive feature. But it is, after all, right in the middle of its face. Traditional bears have embroidered noses of many shapes and sizes. Triangles and ovals are the most popu-lar shapes. You might try cutting out shapes from scraps of black paper or fabric and placing them on the nose area. When you have decided on the nose shape, take a few basting stitches to remind you where the borders are.

Another option to consider, especially if you are making a light-colored bear, is using brown, beige or pink yarn. Most bears, however, look great with the tra-ditional black noses and mouths.

Eyes

Serious Bear   Cross-Eyed Bear   Innocent Bear   Silly Bear   Shy Bear
Close   Too Close   Wide   High   Low

The eyes, of course, are the windows of your teddy bear's soul. Take the eyes you've selected and try placing them on the face. Close-set eyes give the serious look of the original German Steiff bears. But if you get them too close together, your poor bear will be cross-eyed. Wide-set eyes will look innocent and relaxed—some people think they are the most attractive for a bear. Put the eyes down low on the face of a very shy or a very young bear. Put them up higher for a woeful bear or a silly one.

Picture Frame

"When Great-Aunt Sarah Bearnhardt came to visit, we thought her very dramatic," T.R. told Quite A. Small-Bear one day, referring to a prettily framed photo on the parlor table. "Of course, she lived with a little girl in New York City and went to the theater frequently."

Surround the newest member of your family tree with these playful woodland creatures and flowers. Our animal friends are embroidered in crewel yarn on a padded linen picture frame, trimmed with an eyelet ruffle. Exterior measurements are 9⅜ by 11¼ inches plus ¾ inch for the eyelet all around. What a delightful gift for a new mother or proud grandma!

16 by 18" piece off-white linen
Iron, to transfer design on bound-in sheet
3-ply Persian yarn: 9 yards light brown; 4 yards each pink, moss green and dark brown; 3 yards medium brown; 2 yards each off-white, blue and light blue; 1 yard each light purple, beige, gray and gold
6-strand embroidery floss: 1 yard each white, pink and dark brown
Embroidery hoop and crewel needle
1½ yards of ¾"-wide off-white eyelet ruffling
2 or 3 pieces of 9⅜ by 11¼" quilt batting
Off-white sewing thread
7 by 9" piece muslin or other cotton fabric
Heavy cardboard: 1 piece 9⅛ by 11¼", 1 piece 11 by 13"
½ yard solid pink or pink-print fabric
White glue or a 48" length of fusible bonding web
30" length of strong string

Embroidering the Frame

1. Zigzag or overcast edges of linen.

2. Iron motif (see large, bound-in pattern sheet provided) onto linen, centering the motif on the fabric.

3. Insert linen fabric into frame or hoop and work embroidery, following non-transferrable instructions for the stitches and colors, printed in black on the pattern. Stitch diagrams can be found on pages 14 and 15.

4. Cut yarn into 18-inch lengths.

5. Separate yarn and use one-ply for all stitches. Separate floss and use three strands for all stitches.

6. Work long-and-short stitch and satin stitch in direction of arrows. On bears, work tiny lines for fur indicated on pattern using medium running stitches and brown yarn. Use embroidery floss for the features of the animals. For bears' eyes, use white and brown floss and satin stitch; for nose, use brown floss and satin stitch; and for mouth, use pink floss and backstitch. For features of bunny, work the eye using brown floss and one running stitch, the nose in pink floss and satin stitch and mouth in pink floss and backstitch.

Assembling the Frame

1. When needlework is complete, steam-press embroidery on wrong side. Draw a 4⅜- by 6¼-inch rectangle in center of the off-white muslin. Pin muslin to the right side of linen along matching inner rectangle. Baste, then stitch along lines, using between 12 and 15 stitches per inch. Cut center out of both linen and muslin ½ inch from stitching; clip to corners. Turn all fabric in through rectangle; press to wrong side.

2. Sew eyelet around outer edge of embroidery ¼ inch outside pink backstitches; miter corners (see page 36 for directions for mitered corners) so there will be just enough fullness to turn corner when eyelet is folded outward. Stitch ends of eyelet together; zigzag seam allowance. Trim edge 1¼ inches from eyelet; trim corners diagonally. Press under ¼ inch on all edges except corners.

3. Cut a 4⅜- by 6¼-inch opening in center of smaller cardboard piece. Cut two or three pieces of quilt batting using cardboard frame as pattern. Place frame between linen and muslin; attach muslin to back of frame with glue or strips of fusible web. Place batting between cardboard and linen.

4. Fold ends of linen to back side of frame; eyelet should run around edge of cardboard frame. Miter corners; hold edges in place on wrong side with pins. Glue or sew linen to edge of cotton fabric.

Finishing the Back

1. Round the corners of larger cardboard rectangle.

2. Cut a 12½- by 14½-inch piece of pink fabric.

3. Center large cardboard on back of frame; fold edges of pink fabric over cardboard, clipping at corners; fuse or glue in place.

4. Cut a 10¾- by 12½-inch piece of pink fabric with pinking shears, to prevent fraying. Round the corners.

5. Glue or fuse edges in place on the other side of the cardboard.

6. To make a hanger, punch tiny holes through the covered cardboard at each top corner of the frame, about 3 inches from the top edge. (Use something sharp and pointed, such as the tip of a pair of scissors or a needle.) Make second holes ¼ inch below the first. Thread your needle with the string. From back, stitch through holes on one side, then the other. Tie ends in back so string is taut.

7. Place a line of glue around edge of back of top, bottom and one side of embroidered frame just inside eyelet. Place another line about 1½ inches inside the first one. One side stays open so picture may be inserted.

8. Center frame on covered cardboard and press down. Allow glue to dry before placing a photo of your favorite cub inside.

Hand Towels

The pattern is so simple that the embroidery goes fast. Do it on cotton-linen blend dish towels printed with a country-kitchen windowpane check. It looks almost as if the embroidered bears are on the other side of a bright window looking in at you.

"The trick," says Quite A. Small-Bear, "is to stay near enough to the kitchen so you can tell when there are spoons ripe for licking, but still manage to be elsewhere when you hear the dirty pots hit the sink."

Bears-and-Flowers Design

Bears-and-Hearts Design

To get started, see pages 14 and 15 for cross-stitch and embroidery directions.

Separate six-strand embroidery floss and use four strands for embroidering dish towels. In one corner of your towel, plan how many threads you must stitch over to obtain a fairly even cross-stitch with about seven stitches to the inch: On the towels shown here, the stitches were worked over four threads horizontally and five vertically. The stitches are not as even as they would be on Aida cloth but are close. Don't forget to remove your sample stitches.

20 by 30" cotton or cotton-linen blend red-and-white windowpane-check dish towel
6-strand embroidery floss: 2 skeins brown, 2 yards blue, 1 yard each light green, black, red and yellow
Embroidery hoop and needle

If you would like the center of your flowers to fall on the intersection of windowpane stripes, figure out if the spacing between motifs needs to be adjusted to accommodate the pattern on your piece of fabric. There are three bears on this towel, and you'll start with the center bear.

1. Start with brown thread one thread above border—or about 2 inches from 20-inch end—with left toe of center bear. Continue stitching each row of bear according to chart.

2. Work flower in blue and leaves in green in same position on each side of bear. Repeat bear and flower on each side of center embroidery.

3. Following features diagram, embroider eyes and nose on each bear with black thread and satin stitch and mouth with red thread and satin stitch. On center bear, stitch loops of bow with lazy-daisy stitch and yellow thread; use straight stitch for ends and center. Stitch blue bows on side bears.

20 by 30" cotton or cotton-linen blend blue-and-white windowpane-check dish towel
6-strand embroidery floss: 1 skein each brown and red and 1 yard each blue and black
Embroidery hoop and needle

If you wish to center hearts on the windowpane check, figure out if the spacing between the motifs needs to be adjusted to fit your piece of fabric. There are two bears on this towel, and you'll start with the bear that's placed to the left of center.

1. Start one thread above border—or about 2 inches from 20-inch end of towel—with the right foot of bear on left. Continue stitching bear according to chart.

2. Stitch second bear to right of first one. Embroider hearts with red thread on either side of bears.

3. Following features diagram, embroider eyes and nose on each bear with satin stitch and black thread and mouth with satin stitch and red thread. With blue thread, stitch loops of bows with lazy-daisy stitch. Stitch ends and center of bow with straight stitch.

C an't sleep? Count threads, not sheep, and you'll end up with a pillow and a message for anyone who has ever

Crib Pillow

hugged a teddy. Use a counted-thread cross-stitch technique on Aida cloth. Detailed instructions for cross-stitch are on page 15.

1 yard Aida cloth, 14 stitches per inch
Off-white and light-blue sewing thread
6-strand embroidery floss (DMC numbers):
    5 yards brown (433); 2 yards each light brown (840), rose (961), light blue (809); 1 yard each light green (996), yellow (445), lavender (554), pink (3689), peach (353), beige (442), light gold (435) and black
1¼ yards light-blue bias tape
1¼ yards cotton cord for piping
1½ yards off-white eyelet ruffling, 1½" wide
12" zipper
2 pieces of muslin, 10 by 12" each
¼ lb polyester fiberfill
Ruler; embroidery needle; embroidery hoop or frame

Pillow Top

1. Cut a 14- by 16-inch piece of Aida cloth. Zigzag or overcast edges. With fabric held horizontally, measure a horizontal rectangle 9 by 11½ inches in center of fabric, marking corners and edges with pins.

2. Using light-blue thread, baste along outer edge of rectangle through holes between woven squares in fabric. In the same way, mark the vertical and horizontal center with basting stitches. The vertical center is in the center of a stitch worked to one side of the basting

thread. The horizontal center falls between two stitches.

3. Insert fabric in embroidery hoop or frame. Separate floss and use two strands for stitching.

4. Work the bed design in cross-stitch following the chart so that basting threads correspond to centers marked on chart. Outline the sheet and pillowcase with backstitches worked between the holes in the Aida cloth.

5. Work bears' features in black straight stitches on top of cross-stitching.

6. Embroider words above and below bed: Count seven rows from top of bed design. Beginning at center of lower edge of top chart, stitch "I can't bear to," matching vertical center of chart to basting. There are six blank rows between bed design and words above and below bed. In same manner, count seven rows below bed design. Beginning at center of top edge of bottom chart, stitch "sleep without you!" matching vertical center of chart to basting.

7. When embroidery is complete, remove center basting threads. Press embroidery on wrong side. Trim the fabric to ½ inch from outer edge of pillow, which is marked by basting threads.

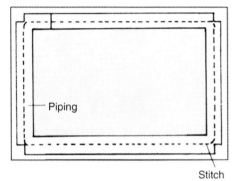

8. For piping, press folds of bias tape open. Fold in half lengthwise and insert cotton cord along fold. Using a zipper foot, stitch along edge of cord. Beginning at lower edge near corner of pillow, baste piping to seam line; stitch again using the zipper foot. Raw edges should extend out. Clip seam allowance to pip-ing when turning corners. Overlap blue bias tape and join ends neatly.

9. Right sides together, baste eyelet ruf-fling around pillow behind piping cord, making a ½-inch pleat on both sides of each corner to add fullness.

Eyelet Ruffling

Pillowcase

1. Cut two 6- by 12¼-inch pieces from Aida cloth for the pillow back. Press under ¼ inch on long edge of one piece. Stitch pressed edge along one side of the zipper a scant ⅛ inch from teeth.

2. Press under ¾ inch on long edge of second piece. Lap over zipper, covering stitching line of first piece. Stitch to other side of zipper tape about ½ inch from fold. Baste across ends of zipper at seam line.

3. Open zipper a few inches. Right sides in, pin pillow back to front; stitch along seam line. Turn pillow right side out.

Inner Pillow

Leaving an opening for turning, stitch muslin pieces together with a ½-inch seam allowance. Turn right side out and stuff pillow with polyester fiberfill so it is smooth and soft. Slip-stitch open-ing closed. Insert pillow into case and zip closed.

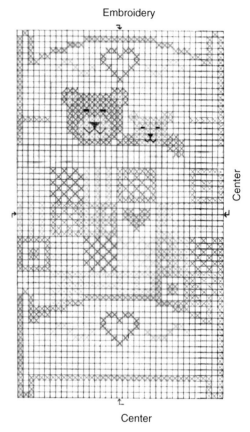

Embroidery

Center

Center

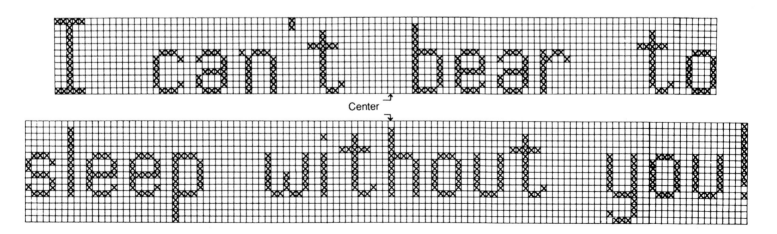

Center

Child & Teddy Twin Set

This pattern is for a child's size 6 but is adaptable to any chest measurement from 23 to 26 inches by adjusting length of body, armholes and sleeves to desired measurement as you work. The garment chest measurement is 27 inches. Directions for a matching teddy bear sweater can be found on page 112.

For a review of knitting stitches and abbreviations, see pages 44 and 45.

Child's Sweater

Knitting worsted yarn: 8 oz or 3 skeins, 3½ oz each MC and hearts (we used Brunswick Germantown Christmas Red), 1 oz white, small amount cinnamon-brown for bears
Sizes 6 and 8 knitting needles or any size that gives you the correct gauge
8 yarn bobbins
2 stitch holders
Yarn or tapestry needle

Determining Correct Gauge

5 sts = 1"; 6 rows = 1". To ensure correct measurements, check your gauge: On size 8 needles, cast on 20 sts and work 24 rows St st. Without bunching or stretching, swatch should be 4" square. If swatch is too small, try again with larger needles; if too large, try smaller needles.

Front

Wind three bobbins with brown yarn, three with white and two with red; set aside for working bear panel. Starting at lower edge, with smaller needles and MC, cast on 68 sts.

Ribbing

Row 1 (Right Side): * K 2, p 2: rep from * across row. Rep same row 11 times more—12 rows (2") in all. Change to larger needles. Work in St st until piece measures 8" from beg or 2" less than desired length to underarm; end with a p row. Attach white; carry MC along side edge. Work 2 rows white, 2 rows MC, 2 rows white. Cut MC, leaving a 6" end.

Bobbins should always hang on purl side of work. When changing colors on a row, bring the new color under previous color to twist yarns and prevent holes in the work. Following the chart below, work rows 2 through 6, adding a white bobbin after each bear on row 4.

Chart for Child's Sweater

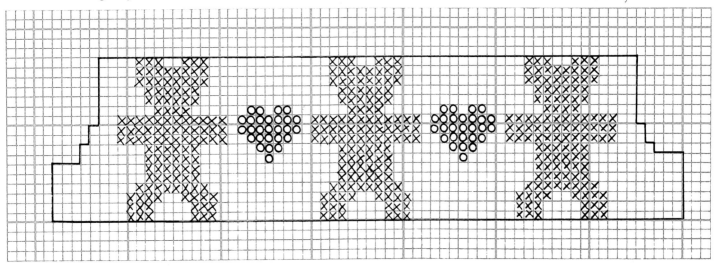

Bear Panel

Row 1: K 8 white. Join first brown bobbin, * k 3 brown; bringing each color across back of work without pulling, k 4 white and 3 brown, drop brown to wrong side, k 11 white; * join 2nd brown bobbin, rep from * to * once, join 3rd brown bobbin, k 3 brown, 4 white, 3 brown, drop brown to wrong side, k 8 white.

Rows 2 Through 6: Foll chart on page 110, work rows adding a white bobbin after each bear on row 4.

Shape Armholes

Bind off 3 sts at beg of chart rows 7 and 8, adding red bobbins for hearts on row 7 (carry white yarn across back of heart as you work heart).

Row 9: SKP (dec made at beg of row), continue foll chart across to last 2 sts, k 2 tog (dec made at end of row).

Row 10: P, foll chart.

Row 11: Dec 1 st each end, as for row 9, foll chart—58 sts. Complete chart; then, cutting off bobbins on first row, leaving 6" ends, work 2 rows white, 2 rows MC, 2 white. Cut white. Continue with MC until armholes measure 3½" above bound-off sts, end with a p row.

Shape Neck

Row 1: K 21, join 2nd ball MC, k 16 and slip to a holder, k 21.

Row 2: P across first side; with next ball of yarn, bind off 2 sts at neck edge on 2nd side, p to end.

Row 3: K across first side; with next ball of yarn, bind off 2 sts; complete row. Continue to work each side separately, dec 1 st at each neck edge every other row 3 times—16 sts each side. Work until armholes measure 6" straight above bound-off sts, ending with a p row.

Shape Shoulders

At each arm edge, bind off 8 sts at beg of every other row, twice.

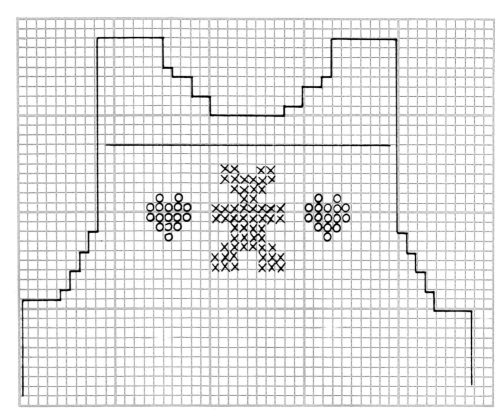

Chart for Teddy Bear's Sweater

Back

With MC, work as for front, omitting stripes, until same length as front to underarms. Bind off 3 sts at beg of next 2 rows; dec 1 st each end of next 2 k rows—58 sts. Work even with MC until same length as front to shoulders. Bind off 8 sts at beg of next 4 rows. Sl rem 26 sts to a holder.

Sleeves

With smaller needles and MC, starting at cuff, cast on 32 sts. Work 12 rows ribbing as for front. Change to larger needles.

Next Row: Inc 1 in first st (to inc, k in front and back of st),* k 9, inc 1 in next st; rep from * ending k 1—36 sts. P 1 row, k 1 row, p 1 row. Continue in St st, inc 1 st each end of every 6th row until there are 48 sts across. Work until sleeves measure 11½" from beg or desired length to underarm.

Shape Cap: Bind off 3 sts at beg of next 2 rows. Dec 1 st each end of every k row 10 times—22 sts. Dec 1 st each end of every row 3 times—16 sts. Bind off 3 sts at beg of next 2 rows. Bind off rem 10 sts.

Finishing

Sew left shoulder seam and neckband. With right side of work facing you, with smaller needles and MC, k 26 from back holder, pick up 19 sts along left neck edge, k 16 from front holder, pick up 19 sts on right neck edge—80 sts. Work in k 2, p 2 ribbing until neckband measures 1". Bind off loosely in ribbing. Weave in ends of yarn on bear panel and sew right shoulder and neckband seam. Pin sweater with right sides tog on padded board or folded towel; pin sleeves flat in same manner; cover with damp towel and let dry. Sew or weave side and sleeve seams. Sew sleeves in place. Weave in ends.

This matching sweater was knitted just for Bearnice Bear. Her measurements are: height, 17 inches; length, 8½ inches; chest girth, 18 inches; and head girth, 17½ inches. So you see that she is a well-proportioned lady bear. Adjust the following instructions if the teddy bear you are going to knit this sweater for has different measurements.

Teddy Bear's Sweater

Knitting worsted yarn: 2¾ oz MC, 1 oz white, small amounts brown and red
Sizes 6 and 8 knitting needles or any sizes that give you the correct gauge
Size F crochet hook
Yarn needle
Stitch holder
¾"-diameter button
4 bobbins (optional)

Bear panel can be knitted in with colors on bobbins or worked in duplicate stitch after the sweater front is completed. The chart for the bear panel for this sweater is on page 111. Gauge for Bearnice's sweater is same as gauge for child's sweater.

Back

With smaller needles and MC, starting at lower edge, cast on 48 sts.

Ribbing
Row 1: K 2, p 2; rep from * across row. Rep this row 3 times more. Change to larger needles. Work in St st for 12 rows, ending with p row. Piece should measure about 2¾" from beg.

Shape Armholes
Bind off 4 sts at beg of next 2 rows.

Next Row (Dec Row): SKP (dec made), k to last 2 sts, k 2 tog (dec made). Rep this row every k row 3 times more—32 sts. P 1 row; k 1 row; p 1 row.

Divide for Opening
Next Row: K 16; sl rem sts to holder. Work 12 rows, ending at center back.

Shape Neck

Row 1: Bind off 5 sts as if to p, p to end.
Row 2: K 11.
Row 3: Bind off 4 sts, p across.
Row 4: K 7.
Row 5: Bind off all sts as to p. Join yarn at center and work other side to correspond, binding off at neck on k rows.

Front

Work as for back until first armhole dec and next p row are completed—38 sts. Join white; cut MC. Continue armhole shaping as for back with white yarn (k in bear and hearts with yarn on bobbins, foll chart (page 111), if desired; when changing colors, twist yarns tog once to prevent holes in work). Complete panel of 15 rows white. Join MC, cut white. Work 3 rows MC.

Shape Neck

Next Row: K 12, sl rem sts to holder. At neck edge, bind off 2 sts at beg of every other row, twice, then dec 1 st once. Work on 7 sts until same length as back to shoulders. Bind off. Leaving center 8 sts on holder, sl last 12 sts to left needle: join red and work to correspond to first side, reversing shaping.

Duplicate Stitch Panel

Each duplicate st covers 1 k st. Foll chart, start at lower left of bear's leg. Thread yarn needle; fasten end of yarn on back of work; insert needle from back to front in base of st to be covered, then from right to left under 2 threads of st above and to back where thread came out—duplicate st made. Work across rows, covering sts as indicated on chart; do not pull too tightly and guide yarn with fingers as you work to cover st completely. Fasten off on wrong side when entire figure is completed. Weave in ends.

Neckband

Sew shoulder seams. With k side of work facing you, using smaller needles and MC, starting at left back neck edge, pick up and k 58 sts around neck, including sts on holder, ending at right back neck corner. Work 3 rows k 2, p 2 ribbing. Bind off loosely in ribbing: Do not cut yarn. Insert crochet hk in lp and work sc at top of back opening, ch 4 for button lp, sk ½" on edge; now sc evenly down one side of back opening and up other side to top of ribbing. Fasten off.

Sleeves

With smaller needles and MC, starting at lower edge, cast on 36 sts. Work 4 rows k 2, p 2 ribbing as for back. Change to larger needles. Work in St st, inc 1 st each end of 5th row, then every 6th row twice—42 sts. P 1 row, k 1 row, p 1 row.

Shape Cap: Bind off 4 sts at beg of next 2 rows. Dec 1 st each end of every other row 8 times—18 sts. P 1 row. Bind off 2 sts at beg of next 2 rows. Bind off rem 14 sts.

Finishing

Centering top of sleeve at shoulder seam, sew sleeve cap to armhole. Sew side and sleeve seams. Sew button opposite lp. Raise bear's arms up and slip sweater over arms and head.